Short a Attack

Name _____

Across
1. a small house, made from logs
4. a fire-breathing animal
5. the home of a king or queen
8. a red fruit

Down
2. a spaceman
3. the horn of a deer
6. a baby frog
7. the opposite of first

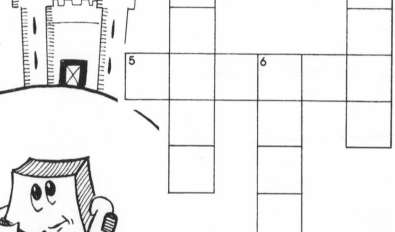

Word Bank

caterpillar	plants	tadpole	castle	last
apple	half	dragon	astronaut	had
cabin	antler	animal	trash	have

Swimming with Short i

Name _____

Across
2. a branch of a tree
3. the root word of missing
4. a sound made with your lips
6. a voyage or journey

Down
1. to leap or jump lightly
2. moving in water
4. the season following fall
5. narrow or skinny

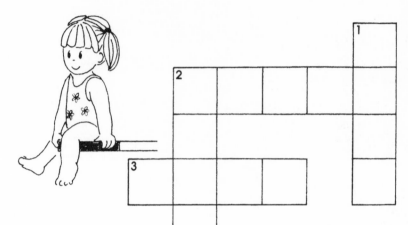

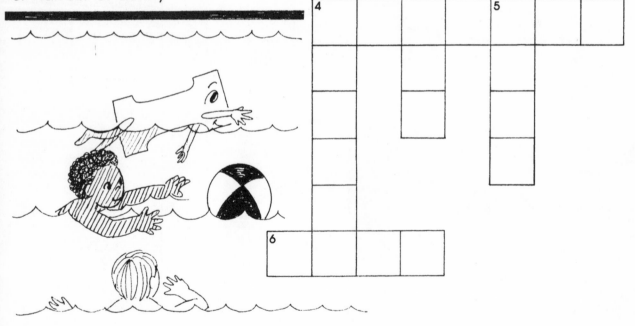

Word Bank

fishing	village	winter	skip	whistle
swimming	million	trip	thin	sixth
quickly	quicksand	miss	spill	stick

The Seven Short e's

Name _____

Across
2. the grade after first grade
5. something taken when you are sick
7. a movie about cowboys and Indians

Down
1. Food gives us _____.
3. to make your body work
4. going down a hill on a sled
6. people or things you speak about

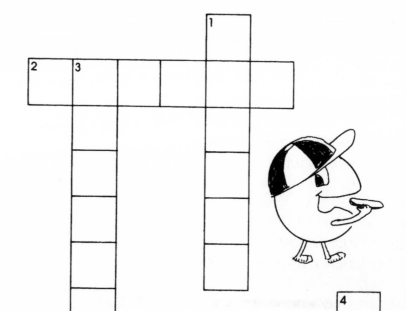

Word Bank

seven	second	jelly	exercise	them
then	getting	western	elephant	sledding
kept	breakfast	special	medicine	energy

The Short o Doctor

Name _____

Across

1. the first bird you see in spring
4. the person who makes you well when you are sick
5. to let something fall
7. a person who steals

Down

2. a baby's toy
3. a baby just learning to walk
6. when it's hard to see outside

Word Bank

ostrich	robber	toddler	chopped	shopping
hopping	bother	foggy	knock	operate
drop	doctor	robin	block	flock

Brushing Up on Short u

Name _____

Across
3. the time just before dark
4. your shortest finger
7. soft candy
8. "bone movers"

Down
1. When something won't move, it is _____.
2. to look for something
5. something held over your head in the rain
6. a group of grapes

Word Bank

bunch	drumstick	fudge	dusk	stuck
bubble	thumb	lunch	hunt	umbrella
muscles	buzz	crush	bumping	understand

Grade A Work!

Name _____

Across

1. where something is located
2. Your tongue is used for this.
4. to run after something
5. traveling in a boat with sails
6. a long reptile with no legs

Down

1. a round, flat dish
3. your class in school
4. something used for coloring a picture

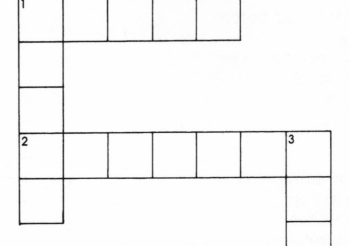

Word Bank

crayon	tasting	chase	plate	player
grade	snake	skating	maybe	making
place	blade	dangerous	angel	sailing

The Long E Beast

Name _____

Across
3. a dairy food
4. 2 + 1 = _____.
6. a noise made by a pig
7. an animal that gives wool

Down
1. a good-manners word
2. a grain that flour is made from
5. to stretch to get something
6. It comes from boiling water.

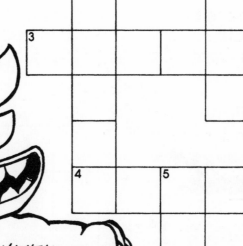
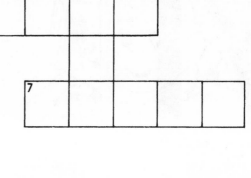
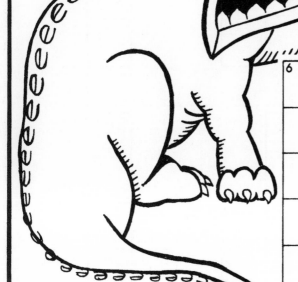

Word Bank

people	deep	leaving	wheat	beast
sheep	steam	teeth	knees	cheese
cleaning	reach	three	please	squeal

Hiding Behind Long I

Name _____

Across
2. making a car go
3. a short time
4. having stripes
7. more dry

Down
1. electricity in the sky
4. a happy face
5. extinct, huge reptile
6. fastened with string

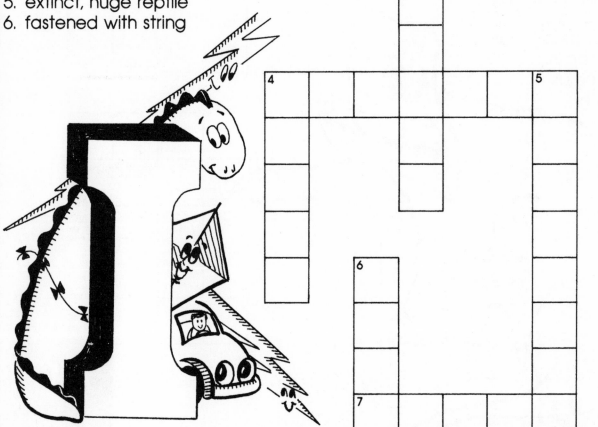

Word Bank

shine	right	driving	lightning	slide
hiding	striped	drier	kites	awhile
write	tied	dinosaur	smile	quiet

8

Bowling with Long O

Name _____

Across
1. a round model of the earth
2. They keep you warm.
4. a small rock
6. not working anymore
7. an animal with rough, brown skin

Down
1. spirits or goblins
3. more cold
5. bread eaten at breakfast

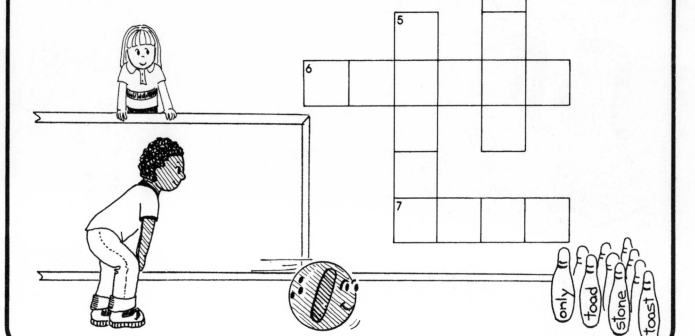

Word Bank

only	bowling	broken	ghosts	toast
hoping	groceries	colder	joking	clothes
toad	floated	globe	stone	roped

Super U

Name _____

Across
2. a student in school
3. an honest answer
5. beautiful sound made by singing
7. to spoil something
8. a long pipe

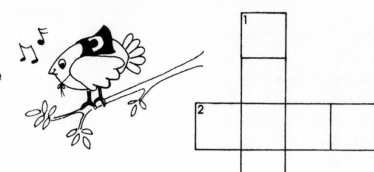

Down
1. apples, oranges, and bananas
4. an imaginary horse-like animal with one horn
6. a set of clothes

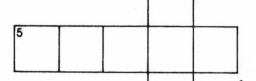

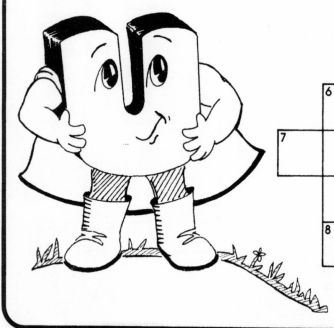

Word Bank

music	unicorn	tuning	fruit	cube
useful	pupil	cuter	glue	suit
bluebird	ruin	human	tube	truth

Compound Crossword

Across
2. perhaps
4. somebody
5. a man made of snow
7. lightning bug

Down
1. to the inside of
3. a sport played with a bat, ball, and glove
5. star-shaped sea animal
6. weight used by weight-lifters

Word Bank

football	birthday	bluejay	maybe	baseball
doghouse	someone	into	snowman	everybody
starfish	barbell	flagpole	firefly	spaceship

11

Blooming Blends

Name _____

Across
3. to shine with quick little lights
4. the funny person in the circus
5. purple or green fruit that grows in a bunch
7. to let go of

Down
1. Put this on a letter for postage.
2. blossoms
5. shining in the dark
6. how you feel when you do something special

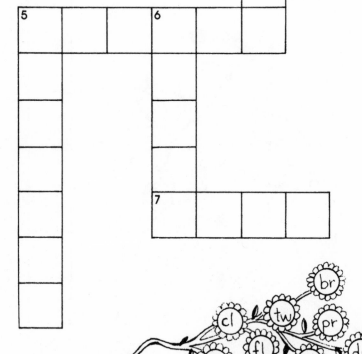

Word Bank

brother	clown	spills	trailed	flowers
black	climb	glowing	twinkle	stamp
front	special	grapes	proud	drop

Sharp Shooters

Name _____

Across
1. a solid dairy food
4. a hen or rooster
6. a little store
7. using something with a friend

Down
2. something worn on your feet
3. the front part of your body, above your waist
5. deciding what you want
7. having a pointed end

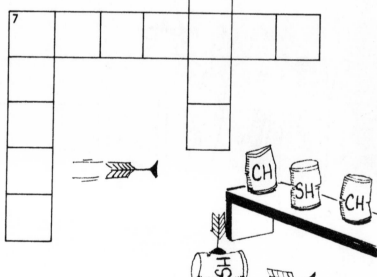

Word Bank

sheep	chopped	chased	ships	should
chewing	shop	choosing	chicken	sharing
children	cheese	sharp	shoes	chest

The "ing" Things

Name _____

Across
3. putting your hands together to make a sound
4. twirling around like a top
6. thinking first about how to do something
7. receiving

Down
1. coming in first place
2. tapping lightly
5. making a quick, sharp sound

Missing E Mystery!

Name _____

Across
4. going from one place to another
6. the opposite of taking
7. clearing leaves away with a tool

Down
1. sitting on something while it is going
2. what you are doing when you give part of your lunch away
3. what the sun is doing
5. moving smoothly on snow or ice

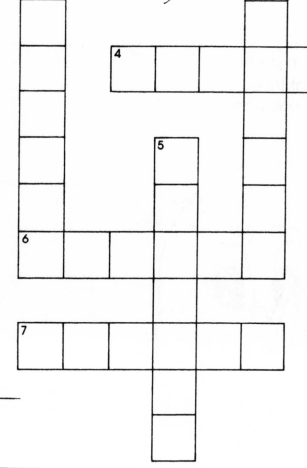

Thumbs Up!

Name _____

Across
1. to use your brain
2. the color of snow
4. to melt snow or ice
6. hairs growing on a man's face
7. A car sits on four of them.

Down
1. needing a drink
3. skinnier
5. to speak very softly
7. asking the reason

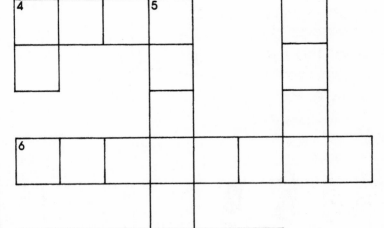

Word Bank

why	that	whiskers	thinner	thumb
thaw	them	white	thimble	thank
what	wheels	think	whisper	thirsty

16

Perfect Pairs

Name _____

Across
4. hugs and _____
5. paper and _____
6. bread and _____
8. sugar and _____

Down
1. _____ and Jill
2. _____ and jelly
3. _____ and bat
7. _____ and socks

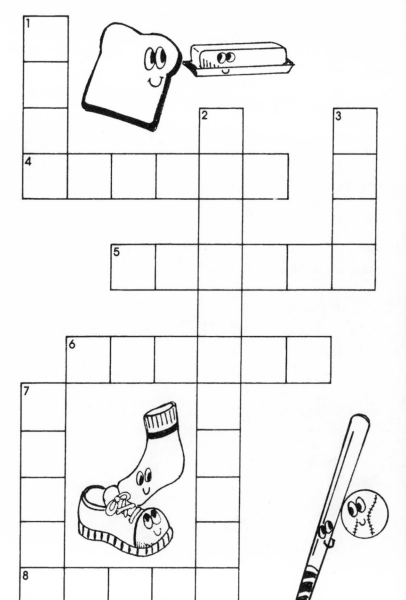

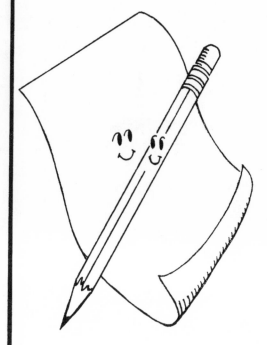

Word Bank

shoes-socks   hugs-kisses   sugar-spice
Mama-Papa   ball-bat   peanut butter-jelly
bread-butter   paper-pencil
stars-stripes   Jack-Jill

Math Adds Up to Fun!

Across
3. how much something is worth
4. each of two numbers you add together
6. In 27, the 2 is in the _____ place.
8. the symbol for a number

Down
1. In 201, the 2 is in the _____ place.
2. to take away, as 5 - 3 = 2
5. the sign =
7. the answer you get when you add
9. to put numbers together, as 9 + 6 = 15

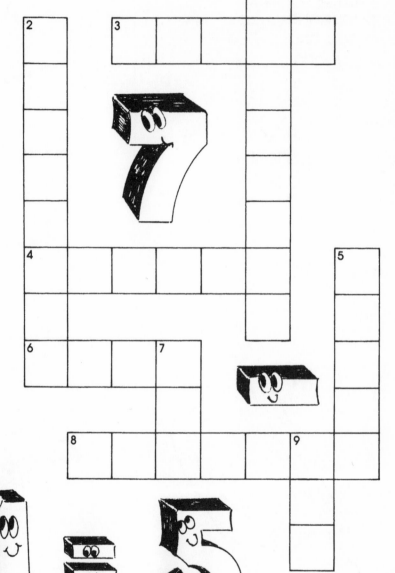

Word Bank

add	sum	equal	less	value
subtract	fewer	numeral	hundreds	ones
problem	greater	addend	tens	cent

School Tools

Name _____

Across
1. sheets of paper fastened together
2. class in school
4. used to remove pencil marks
6. colors to mix with a brush and water

Down
1. a person who teaches
2. helps stick things together
3. a colored, waxy stick used for drawing
5. a tool used for cutting
6. a sheet to write or draw on

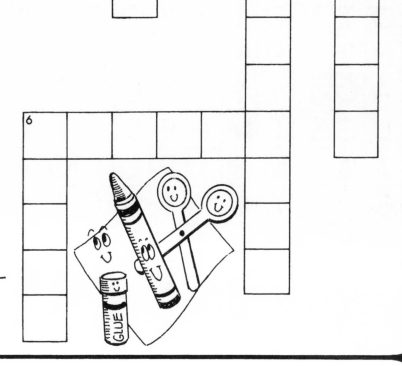

Word Bank

pencil	school	tablet	desk	paper
book	glue	brush	teacher	paints
apple	scissors	crayon	grade	eraser

A Is a Blast!

Help this rocket blast-off from its launching pad by circling the **short a words**.

C	L	P	L	A	N	T	S	R	O	D	W	T
S	A	F	P	A	R	Y	L	E	E	A	O	P
F	L	A	T	R	T	A	D	P	O	L	E	T
O	S	U	N	B	U	L	E	X	S	L	I	O
A	I	N	S	O	C	T	M	E	H	A	L	F
S	D	R	O	F	N	W	D	R	A	G	O	N
T	T	H	E	D	C	N	A	L	R	T	I	C
R	H	A	G	O	A	H	U	Y	Z	B	O	L
O	T	V	O	I	S	B	O	C	A	B	I	N
N	P	E	R	N	T	S	N	A	C	I	M	O
A	O	T	I	S	L	T	U	N	R	I	R	Y
U	C	L	E	M	E	P	S	T	A	L	E	N
T	A	L	M	P	I	R	L	L	O	A	Q	T
Q	K	P	A	C	K	T	A	E	T	S	W	R
S	P	O	F	G	W	I	L	R	N	T	B	A
A	A	N	I	M	A	L	O	P	E	S	O	S
C	A	T	E	R	P	I	L	L	A	R	O	H

Word Bank

flat	half	cabin	castle	tadpole
last	have	plants	antler	astronaut
pack	trash	dragon	animal	caterpillar

In the Swim!

Name _____

Dip in and swim.
Circle the **short i words** in blue.

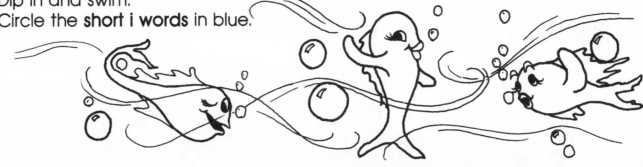

W	G	N	S	F	R	I	L	O	G	S	K	I	P	F	L
I	O	S	V	I	L	L	A	G	E	I	J	M	A	S	T
N	U	M	A	S	W	I	L	P	V	N	O	I	Q	U	R
T	Q	I	T	H	E	L	Q	U	I	C	K	L	Y	S	I
E	U	S	V	I	U	M	U	N	C	B	G	L	O	P	P
R	A	S	T	N	I	W	I	W	T	E	R	I	F	L	P
W	O	I	A	G	N	S	C	I	P	Q	S	O	S	G	E
A	U	N	Z	O	L	I	K	M	I	A	I	N	H	M	D
V	M	G	I	H	E	S	S	O	C	P	B	N	S	L	D
I	K	O	M	A	W	I	A	G	K	R	S	P	I	L	L
H	S	W	I	M	M	I	N	G	T	M	S	G	X	O	B
S	V	N	U	R	E	P	D	V	A	G	O	O	T	D	L
T	H	I	N	N	E	R	P	A	W	H	I	C	H	E	R

Word Bank

fishing	village	which	missing	thinner
swimming	million	winter	sixth	spill
quickly	quicksand	tripped	skip	pick

"Best in the West"

Name_____

E	M	O	W	L	E	N	E	R	G	Y	K	N
L	R	D	E	O	S	A	T	S	E	V	E	N
E	T	A	S	E	T	Y	R	E	J	A	P	I
P	H	L	T	N	O	M	L	C	U	J	T	A
H	E	B	E	Y	G	Y	K	O	D	E	X	S
A	M	A	R	E	T	H	E	N	W	L	C	L
N	G	B	N	Q	O	S	L	D	C	L	G	E
T	J	I	K	E	M	Y	I	T	S	Y	A	D
B	E	X	E	R	C	I	S	E	N	Y	E	D
R	G	E	R	A	T	A	L	Q	F	Q	U	I
D	B	V	O	H	O	I	H	R	P	A	N	N
T	F	B	R	E	A	K	F	A	S	T	O	G
I	W	M	I	J	R	R	G	H	F	E	S	K
D	V	T	I	F	C	G	E	T	T	I	N	G
E	L	S	B	R	O	E	L	I	W	O	A	N
T	S	P	E	C	I	A	L	X	N	T	M	L
S	C	B	R	M	E	D	I	C	I	N	E	E

Word Bank

seven	them	breakfast	western	exercise
then	second	sledding	special	elephant
kept	getting	jelly	energy	medicine

Sock Hop

Name_____

Sock it to me! Circle the **short o words** in the puzzle.

T	O	H	O	P	P	I	N	G	R	E	S	A	L	W	I
A	B	L	E	R	B	C	H	O	P	P	E	D	A	S	L
S	O	C	T	O	Z	W	A	G	R	I	R	L	M	H	A
E	T	A	O	P	D	R	O	P	P	E	D	N	C	O	I
C	H	L	D	O	E	J	S	V	I	W	X	A	N	P	O
O	E	X	D	I	B	N	T	A	R	O	M	F	E	P	L
R	R	S	L	E	L	O	R	O	R	E	B	X	N	I	A
O	P	T	E	K	O	S	I	A	O	H	J	L	I	N	O
B	D	E	R	L	C	B	C	O	B	W	F	O	G	G	Y
I	A	O	F	C	K	A	H	R	B	B	L	I	F	W	A
N	U	X	A	L	I	O	T	S	E	O	O	B	E	L	N
M	J	S	C	D	O	C	T	O	R	M	C	A	L	E	I
O	P	E	R	A	T	E	P	A	Z	W	K	N	O	C	K

Word Bank

ostrich	shopping	operate	robin	knock
hopping	robber	toddler	flock	block
dropped	bother	foggy	chopped	doctor

Just Ducky!

Name_____

B	A	K	B	U	B	B	L	E	L	O	I	S
U	S	M	G	O	K	L	A	R	T	D	M	B
M	G	U	D	I	T	E	U	S	J	R	O	U
P	M	N	D	A	H	S	A	T	L	U	A	N
I	T	D	E	R	U	W	U	U	O	M	I	C
N	E	E	X	O	M	G	A	C	L	S	B	H
G	O	R	L	E	B	F	L	K	A	T	M	E
W	I	S	O	K	U	N	I	M	E	I	C	K
M	L	T	N	O	R	D	Z	U	L	C	A	Y
B	I	A	R	F	K	U	W	M	N	K	Y	U
I	S	N	A	L	C	S	R	B	E	A	I	B
F	U	D	G	E	D	K	I	R	L	L	R	U
O	B	R	I	S	A	R	O	E	V	U	O	Z
S	C	C	R	U	S	H	A	L	S	N	K	Z
M	X	E	T	O	R	R	T	L	N	C	T	I
M	U	S	C	L	E	F	H	A	K	H	L	N
G	A	H	U	N	T	E	D	N	M	C	S	G

Jump in and circle the **short u words.**

Watch out for the puddles!

Word Bank

bunch	stuck	muscle	lunch	dusk
bubble	drumstick	umbrella	buzzing	hunted
understand	thumb	fudge	bumping	crush

24

Train Game

Name_____

Stop, look, and listen for the **long a words** in the puzzle. Circle them.

M	A	D	U	T	L	P	R	P	L	A	T	E	V	E	S
C	I	G	R	A	D	E	H	L	O	K	V	A	F	H	C
A	M	C	B	S	O	N	M	A	C	D	H	E	R	A	F
L	A	Q	S	T	H	B	A	Y	J	Y	B	L	A	D	E
C	K	A	E	I	M	W	P	E	R	G	D	Y	M	V	L
E	I	N	L	N	C	D	O	R	A	E	M	A	E	D	C
S	N	U	G	L	O	B	K	N	C	W	S	E	A	H
M	G	E	P	U	F	S	N	A	K	E	O	A	Z	L	A
A	F	L	E	C	G	O	A	K	Y	E	B	I	L	H	S
Y	T	G	S	K	A	T	I	N	G	X	K	L	A	O	E
B	A	W	N	F	V	I	W	L	H	E	O	I	T	S	D
E	R	D	A	N	G	E	R	O	U	S	R	N	A	T	V
C	Z	N	O	C	R	A	Y	O	N	U	M	G	L	A	D

Word Bank

crayon	player	blade	skating	plate
grade	tasting	making	dangerous	maybe
frame	snake	chased	sailing	angel

Sweet Treats

Name_____

D	E	E	P	A	C	E	C	T	E	E	T	H
C	S	W	A	T	L	S	O	L	A	E	Q	I
C	M	E	M	F	E	U	S	R	R	O	P	A
H	A	S	T	E	A	M	O	B	E	Z	E	L
E	G	C	H	R	N	J	G	L	A	I	O	B
E	H	O	R	A	I	B	T	E	C	V	P	S
S	M	I	E	C	N	P	D	W	H	F	L	X
E	H	R	E	A	G	Y	T	D	I	I	E	O
M	S	P	A	T	O	G	U	R	N	G	U	J
A	M	B	K	E	L	G	W	I	G	K	P	I
S	H	E	E	P	U	H	A	C	B	A	K	S
W	E	A	L	J	S	L	E	A	V	I	N	G
C	I	S	W	N	B	E	I	P	A	P	E	M
V	I	T	O	E	F	S	F	O	S	U	E	I
T	U	O	S	Q	U	E	A	L	H	A	S	T
V	B	U	I	S	O	L	N	R	C	E	P	M
J	P	L	E	A	S	E	R	W	H	E	A	T

Word Bank

people	beast	reaching	teeth	wheat
sheep	deep	cheese	three	knees
cleaning	steam	leaving	squeal	please

Flying High!

Name _____

Flying high in the sky,
Looking for the **words with long i.**
Circle them.

F	S	I	B	L	K	I	T	E	S	A	N	M	I	U	L
L	Y	S	G	R	L	L	V	C	Q	J	I	H	N	E	F
I	E	T	S	A	H	Y	A	P	S	M	N	I	B	F	I
G	R	W	H	I	D	I	N	G	O	G	T	S	W	R	N
H	W	E	I	H	G	A	O	Y	B	R	H	P	R	L	D
T	K	G	N	I	M	Q	P	D	E	I	O	S	I	P	I
N	O	A	E	B	T	U	H	I	L	G	I	A	T	O	N
I	D	M	A	G	J	I	K	N	E	H	S	F	E	U	G
N	M	L	E	R	O	T	I	O	U	T	M	I	G	T	H
G	E	S	M	I	L	E	N	S	O	S	B	A	C	A	I
L	V	S	O	H	R	G	E	A	H	S	T	R	I	P	E
O	X	S	L	I	D	E	F	U	S	F	X	I	Z	P	T
D	R	I	V	I	N	G	A	R	Y	A	Q	U	I	E	T

Word Bank

shine	slide	quite	ninth	lightning
hiding	right	finding	dinosaur	kites
write	stripe	driving	quiet	smile

Ghost Hosts!

Name_____

F	E	L	G	H	O	S	T	S	Z	I	H	O
L	T	N	A	L	P	E	R	P	O	F	O	N
O	G	T	O	A	D	L	E	N	F	A	P	Y
A	X	S	I	U	O	C	H	T	A	P	I	O
T	Y	P	O	B	A	L	Z	O	E	O	N	B
E	G	O	V	O	N	O	I	A	H	S	G	N
D	O	M	G	W	A	T	Z	S	H	I	A	T
E	N	B	O	L	G	H	L	T	U	W	F	L
R	L	W	G	I	H	E	V	S	T	O	N	E
I	Y	C	R	N	X	S	A	L	B	W	A	N
Z	O	G	E	G	R	O	C	E	R	I	E	S
O	U	L	H	W	S	I	W	R	O	O	P	L
T	N	O	D	B	R	O	K	E	N	B	G	R
F	L	B	A	U	C	O	L	D	E	R	K	O
S	N	E	U	G	M	R	B	O	N	L	D	P
B	H	G	J	O	K	I	N	G	O	V	A	E
R	I	S	P	E	L	K	V	R	A	M	O	D

Most ghosts are noble hosts. They'll float and boast, From coast to coast, About the ghost Who finds the most. Finds what? Why, the **long o words**. Now you find them and circle them.

Word Bank

only	toast	floated	colder	ghosts
hoping	bowling	clothes	globe	joking
toad	groceries	broken	roped	stone

Super Fruit

Name _____

These super-duper fruits have super powers. Use their powers to find the **long u words**. Circle them in blue.

S	A	U	T	G	R	F	O	I	P	H	I	S	U	I	T
T	U	N	I	C	O	R	N	O	U	I	P	N	D	O	W
U	G	N	R	I	C	U	H	P	P	J	M	U	S	I	C
T	H	B	I	U	T	I	K	I	I	A	L	I	O	F	U
U	L	L	F	U	N	T	G	L	L	V	A	N	N	U	B
N	N	U	C	I	O	E	T	B	Y	T	U	B	E	O	E
I	G	E	N	Z	H	U	M	A	N	W	O	G	N	I	R
N	L	B	U	Z	S	C	P	A	E	U	N	S	C	U	R
G	N	I	S	D	L	N	A	U	S	E	F	U	L	I	U
D	U	R	F	N	Y	I	F	A	U	W	G	B	X	M	I
V	P	D	T	O	C	U	T	E	R	N	I	T	L	W	N
R	A	C	D	M	U	E	V	D	I	R	T	R	U	T	H
T	N	E	M	Y	G	L	U	E	O	P	S	A	E	M	O

Word Bank

music	cube	ruin	cuter	fruit
useful	unicorn	suit	human	glue
bluebird	pupil	tuning	truth	tube

Compound Hound!

Name_____

Put your nose to the ground and "sniff" out these compound words.

D	M	E	V	E	R	Y	B	O	D	Y	A	B
O	C	I	C	U	P	C	A	K	E	M	S	A
G	L	Y	Z	B	L	U	E	J	A	Y	B	S
H	T	S	U	I	A	I	R	P	L	A	N	E
O	R	O	N	S	P	A	S	Y	R	O	P	B
U	O	M	D	O	W	S	H	I	E	T	L	A
S	S	E	O	M	F	O	O	T	B	A	L	L
E	L	T	N	E	N	M	S	T	I	W	C	L
L	O	H	L	O	A	I	K	J	R	E	M	T
S	M	I	W	N	T	S	S	E	T	I	A	F
N	O	N	S	E	N	I	E	I	H	S	C	I
O	U	G	T	P	O	L	S	N	D	H	E	R
W	F	D	S	L	F	V	M	M	A	H	S	E
M	G	I	B	N	O	B	O	D	Y	E	S	F
A	L	C	T	J	S	K	S	P	O	N	I	L
N	S	F	L	A	G	P	O	L	E	E	I	Y
C	E	B	S	P	A	C	E	S	H	I	P	C

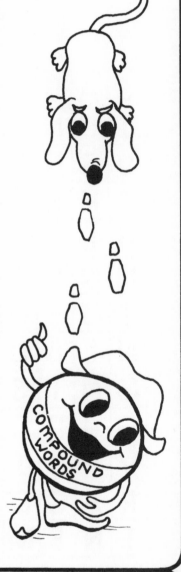

Word Bank

football	baseball	nobody	flagpole	snowman
doghouse	birthday	everybody	spaceship	firefly
cupcake	someone	something	airplane	bluejay

Blending Bloomers

Name_____

Blending Bloomers will blush and blossom as you circle these words with blooming blends. Circle the **blends** in blue or black.

C	R	L	I	B	G	S	O	A	C	A	B	L	I	G	N		
A	B	T	Y	O	P	N	W	G	L	O	W	I	N	G	S		
F	L	O	W	E	R	S	A	I	I	M	E	R	F	S	P		
D	A	W	O	N	S	P	C	E	M	H	O	M	T	U	R		
U	C	B	W	N	V	E	I	G	B	U	K	L	G	I	O		
P	K	E	C	S	S	C	O	D	R	O	O	P	N	G	U		
O	R	O	F	R	E	I	B	I	E	Y	N	S	W	T	D		
I	S	B	O	T	R	A	I	L	O	D	K	W	O	G	L		
G	P	M	C	E	K	L	G	A	D	O	M	C	H	R	Y		
F	I	O	L	I	A	L	F	R	O	N	T	S	I	A	T		
U	L	H	O	O	S	T	A	M	P	T	A	I	C	P	O		
P	L	Q	W	R	S	A	E	D	B	R	O	T	H	E	R		
F	S	S	N	T	W	I	N	K	L	E	B	E	I	S	G		

Word Bank

brother	flowers	stamp	glowing	trail
black	clown	spills	grapes	twinkle
front	climb	special	droop	proudly

Choose New Shoes! Name _____

Choosing new shoes is a chance for a change. Check the shop shelves for **ch/sh** words.

O	S	H	A	R	I	N	G	U	G	C	B	O
C	H	T	A	E	D	Y	L	P	I	H	S	K
H	I	E	W	A	M	C	H	E	W	I	N	G
Y	P	I	R	C	E	N	L	O	I	L	D	A
F	S	O	R	C	H	O	P	P	E	D	O	H
C	M	I	E	H	Y	O	Q	B	A	R	S	G
H	S	E	S	A	K	S	U	S	I	E	H	C
I	O	M	U	S	C	Z	A	H	P	N	E	H
C	H	A	I	E	G	N	S	A	V	I	S	O
K	O	R	V	D	E	M	T	R	B	N	H	O
E	Z	U	V	I	G	T	E	P	L	I	O	S
N	G	S	H	E	E	P	C	H	E	N	P	I
L	F	H	N	O	C	H	Y	E	A	T	P	N
A	W	O	H	C	H	E	E	S	E	L	I	G
E	G	U	S	A	Q	G	D	E	H	U	N	P
V	I	L	G	E	S	H	O	E	S	V	G	W
O	V	D	H	E	T	I	C	C	H	E	S	T

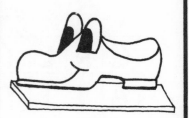

Word Bank

sheep	should	cheese	sharp	ships
chewing	chopped	sharing	choosing	chicken
children	shopping	chased	chest	shoes

Double Bubbles!

Name_____

Double your fun by circling the **words** **with double consonants.** Then use a crayon to circle just the **root word.**

A	S	C	C	O	B	A	R	U	N	N	I	N	G	O	J
H	W	A	L	M	E	I	W	M	O	P	Q	Z	I	N	G
O	I	C	A	I	G	O	R	P	N	A	S	T	O	D	E
P	M	S	P	B	I	S	P	I	N	N	I	N	G	U	T
P	M	Y	P	I	N	V	O	L	I	A	D	G	H	G	T
I	I	O	I	P	N	M	E	G	O	N	A	M	W	E	I
N	N	V	N	E	I	P	O	P	P	I	N	G	I	O	N
G	G	Y	G	P	N	O	X	S	K	O	A	T	N	R	G
F	S	A	N	S	G	M	S	L	E	D	D	I	N	G	O
T	R	I	P	P	I	N	G	O	R	C	K	G	I	E	M
C	O	M	G	E	S	I	T	T	I	N	G	I	N	C	E
E	B	E	R	T	B	O	P	A	T	T	I	N	G	K	J
P	L	A	N	N	I	N	G	Y	L	E	T	T	I	N	G

Word Bank

swimming	spinning	getting	letting	patting
planning	sledding	clapping	winning	sitting
beginning	running	hopping	tripping	popping

Up, Up, and Away!

Name_____

The final **e** in each of these words has blown away to make room for **ing**. Find the **ing words** in the wordsearch.

G	A	C	H	I	D	I	N	G	S	I	O	Y
I	S	T	A	W	O	R	A	F	S	S	E	V
V	O	P	V	I	F	N	E	M	I	L	A	L
I	P	E	I	A	D	S	H	A	K	I	N	G
N	C	I	N	A	C	E	C	K	H	D	E	O
G	R	C	G	U	O	R	C	I	L	I	U	M
M	I	B	C	E	M	Y	W	N	B	N	V	O
A	D	S	L	S	I	B	A	G	P	G	L	V
I	I	H	E	S	N	C	N	E	O	M	S	I
T	N	I	C	K	G	J	O	R	N	A	J	N
R	G	N	N	A	H	I	E	W	P	S	O	G
A	X	I	S	H	A	R	I	N	G	A	K	U
K	I	N	V	E	L	U	T	W	E	S	I	T
I	U	G	M	L	F	P	O	R	A	T	N	I
N	G	I	D	R	I	V	I	N	G	S	G	E
G	I	D	A	N	C	I	N	G	U	D	T	O
P	U	G	C	I	G	N	O	S	X	K	Y	E

Word Bank

sliding	having	riding	giving	joking
shaking	making	moving	sharing	dancing
hiding	driving	coming	raking	shining

"Dear Deer..."

Name _____

Dear Deer,
   I'm trying to write right to tell you to circle these **homonyms**.
      Sincerely,
      Aunt Ant

B	L	U	E	A	C	J	D	W	R	I	T	E	S	T	O
L	W	I	N	T	E	L	A	Y	I	P	Y	L	X	W	E
E	I	A	L	A	N	P	B	O	G	U	T	T	O	O	C
W	D	S	E	N	T	P	S	D	H	E	C	R	A	L	B
S	E	G	P	M	I	M	N	O	T	B	A	S	B	E	E
S	A	L	E	Y	K	N	O	W	S	I	T	C	G	S	K
A	M	D	O	H	I	U	S	L	O	U	E	I	G	H	T
I	C	W	H	A	I	R	E	O	R	T	T	A	E	M	H
L	O	N	T	R	O	U	N	D	T	H	E	I	R	P	W
H	W	I	A	E	K	H	S	B	C	E	N	S	E	E	O
B	Y	M	U	A	B	A	R	E	L	R	M	E	Q	F	U
U	C	P	N	L	W	D	C	A	G	E	O	A	B	S	L
Y	A	N	T	S	R	O	B	R	V	I	K	W	O	O	D

Word Bank

blue-blew	by-buy	wood-would	hair-hare	ant-aunt
nose-knows	their-there	ate-eight	bare-bear	sale-sail
two-too-to	see-sea	be-bee	right-write	cent-sent

Think About This!

Name_____

B	Q	N	O	L	V	X	J	T	T	A	D	O
W	T	H	I	M	B	L	E	J	H	Z	P	W
R	U	H	W	A	O	L	G	Q	I	U	I	H
T	I	F	T	M	Z	C	T	U	N	F	Y	I
H	P	W	H	E	E	L	O	G	N	S	Q	S
U	V	H	N	H	C	K	Z	M	E	C	B	K
M	D	P	W	O	D	Y	A	F	R	L	N	E
B	F	E	H	E	B	S	Y	G	C	R	B	R
O	B	K	A	S	E	T	H	I	N	K	J	U
X	Z	T	T	U	O	W	D	K	L	U	D	A
M	B	O	J	I	F	V	T	H	A	N	K	H
W	H	I	S	P	E	R	I	D	R	M	R	T
H	K	L	U	C	M	L	G	A	G	T	R	H
E	W	T	A	L	H	T	N	Q	S	H	S	E
N	Q	H	I	W	P	W	H	I	T	E	O	M
A	Y	A	K	V	F	O	E	Z	M	R	C	U
J	X	T	O	P	W	H	Y	O	T	E	N	U

Think about which of these **words begin with th or wh.** Where are they? Find them in the wordsearch.

Word Bank

why	that	wheel	thank	thinner
when	them	think	there	whisker
what	thumb	white	thimble	whisper

Prize-Winning Pairs

Name_____

Find these first-place **pairs**. Circle.

J	A	C	K	O	M	T	C	O	J	E	J	I
I	P	E	A	N	U	T	B	U	T	T	E	R
L	G	H	D	E	B	O	L	O	Y	C	L	S
L	T	U	S	T	R	I	P	E	S	N	L	B
S	I	B	T	G	D	M	H	F	M	I	Y	K
N	R	F	A	U	P	E	N	C	I	L	E	C
Y	P	E	R	R	A	P	O	M	X	G	L	O
W	A	M	S	T	P	S	P	E	L	S	X	O
I	P	W	G	R	E	Y	F	N	M	I	L	K
M	A	M	A	K	R	E	X	D	J	I	R	I
B	X	H	L	W	F	W	A	S	K	S	B	E
M	B	M	B	A	T	E	C	H	P	I	J	S
L	U	R	A	Q	V	D	S	O	C	K	S	U
A	T	Y	L	C	A	G	K	E	N	U	M	H
D	T	U	L	N	H	M	V	S	C	H	C	U
X	E	V	C	O	W	Q	A	Z	P	L	H	G
B	R	E	A	D	B	E	K	I	S	S	E	S

Word Bank

hugs-kisses   bat-ball   stars-stripes   peanut butter-jelly

milk-cookies   Jack-Jill   shoes-socks   paper-pencil

bread-butter   Mama-Papa

Math Matters!

Name _____

Math is "sum" fun!
Find the **math words**
in this wordsearch.

B	O	Z	S	W	U	S	G	E	F	I	R	S	T	X	V	S
K	U	H	U	N	D	R	E	D	N	G	S	F	M	E	R	U
M	O	L	M	W	O	B	Q	S	P	N	U	K	N	D	F	B
O	T	U	R	M	I	T	Y	H	R	D	V	A	L	U	E	T
H	I	L	Q	J	G	P	R	F	O	F	T	K	E	H	M	R
B	A	D	D	E	N	D	K	A	B	P	L	O	Q	A	L	A
T	V	R	S	T	I	J	J	E	L	C	E	N	R	D	U	C
R	I	K	T	T	C	O	E	D	E	M	S	D	H	D	L	T
J	T	Z	E	H	E	K	Q	G	M	P	S	M	P	L	Y	E
O	H	F	N	O	T	L	U	M	Y	K	B	F	E	W	E	R
I	R	X	S	N	A	T	A	Z	M	A	N	P	W	K	L	O
W	E	C	B	H	Y	Z	L	I	T	G	R	E	A	T	E	R
B	E	M	N	U	M	E	R	A	L	J	C	X	U	C	B	A

Word Bank

add	less	fewer	addend	subtract
sum	value	three	greater	hundred
tens	first	equal	problem	numeral

School Is Cool!

Name _____

Off to school to find these words,
Up and down, they're words you've heard.

C	A	P	E	N	C	I	L	O	B	N	I	A	T	N	B
K	T	I	P	G	A	Z	S	A	G	L	U	E	U	R	O
T	A	B	L	E	T	B	Q	E	R	U	D	T	I	S	O
L	Y	U	O	M	A	G	D	C	A	S	P	T	V	B	K
A	W	V	F	R	G	R	A	D	E	C	O	E	B	W	E
E	F	G	Y	A	S	M	P	I	L	I	T	A	R	B	P
S	C	H	O	O	L	B	P	N	E	S	L	C	U	Y	A
K	E	T	U	A	C	H	L	U	S	S	O	H	S	A	P
D	C	A	B	I	S	I	E	B	C	O	U	E	H	G	E
E	S	R	F	O	V	E	K	O	B	R	I	R	G	C	R
S	I	M	V	F	P	A	I	N	T	S	G	W	A	B	K
K	F	E	E	C	I	R	I	T	L	E	O	F	H	A	U
X	P	O	C	R	A	Y	O	N	P	E	R	A	S	E	R

Word Bank

pencil	paper	scissors	brush	desk
book	school	paints	crayon	teacher
apple	glue	tablet	eraser	grade

HEAP GOOD!

Name _____

Use words from the Word Bank to finish the riddle. Then use the same words to complete the puzzle.

Question

What do you call a

④➡ _ _ _ _ _ _ _ _

①⬇ _ _ _ _ _ _ _ _ ?

Answer

A ③➡ _ _ _ _ _ _ _

②⬇ _ _ _ _ _ _ _ !

Word Bank

ghostly	teepee	haunted	cat
wigwam	scared	creepy	sheet

MUMMY MADNESS

Name_____

Use words from the
Word Bank to finish
the riddle. Then use
the same words to
complete the puzzle.

Question

How can ③⬇ ___ ___ ___

tell if

④➡ ___ ___ ___ ___ ___

have ②➡ ___ ___ ___ ___ ___ ?

Answer

They ⑤⬇ ___ ___ ___ ___

①⬇ ___ ___ ___ ___ ___ ___ .

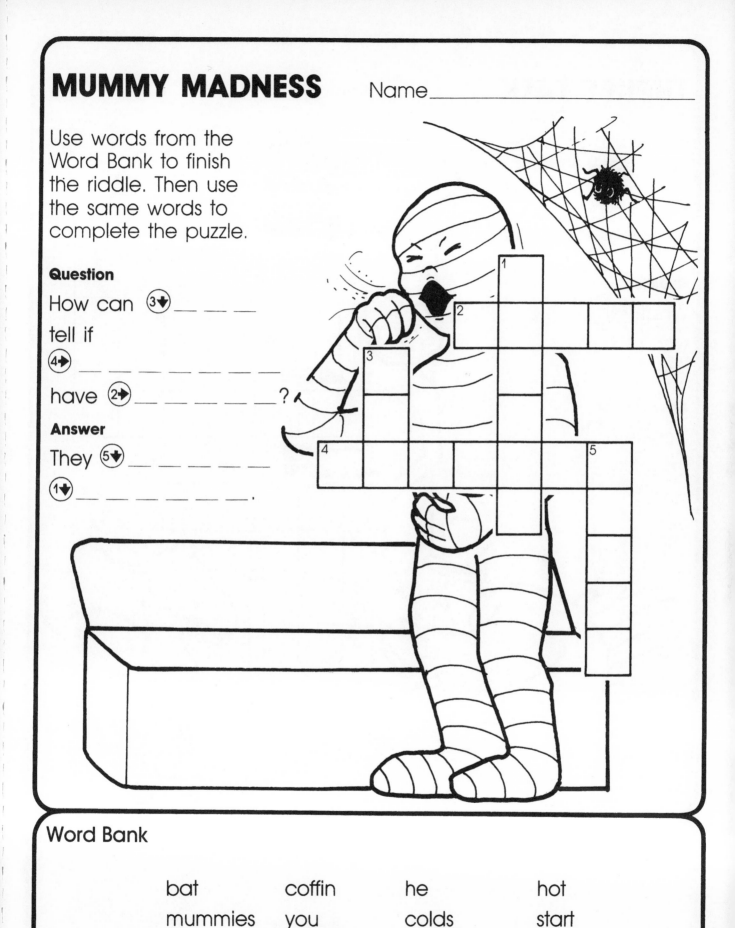

Word Bank

bat	coffin	he	hot
mummies	you	colds	start

TURKEY TALK

Name_____

Use words from the Word Bank to finish the riddle. Then use the same words to complete the puzzle.

Question

What ②⬇ __ __ __ __

won't ⑤⬇ __ __ __ __ __

④➡ __ __ __ __ __ ?

Answer

Don-keys,

③➡ __ __ __ __ __ - __ __ __ __ ,

and

①⬇ __ __ __ __ - __ __ __ __ __ !

Word Bank

money	monkeys	keys	Indian
turkeys	open	teepee	doors

STICKY BUSINESS

Name_____

Use words from the Word Bank to finish the riddle. Then use the same words to complete the puzzle.

Question

What do you get when

you cross

⑤➡ _ _ _ _ _ _

butter with a

②⬇ _ _ _ _ _ _ ?

Answer

A turkey that

①➡ _ _ _ _ _ _

to the roof of

③➡ _ _ _ _

④⬇ _ _ _ _ _ .

Word Bank

thanks	turkey	Pilgrim	sticks
mouth	peanut	jelly	your

MERRY "KISS"-MOOSE!

Name _____

Use words from the Word Bank to finish the riddle. Then use the same words to complete the puzzle.

Question

Why did the

②➡ _ _ _ _ _ _ get

④➡ _ _ _ _ _ on

③⬇ _ _ _ _ _ _ _ _ _?

Answer

He was

⑤⬇ _ _ _ _ _ _ _ _

under the

①⬇ _ _ _ _ _ _ _ _ _ -toe!

Word Bank

angel	Santa	kissed	moostle
moose	Christmas	candle	standing

'TWAS THE NIGHT BEFORE CHRISTMAS...

Name_____

Use words from the Word Bank to finish the riddle. Then use the same words to complete the puzzle.

Question

What (5➡) _ _ _ _ _ _

do (1⬇) _ _ _ _ _ _ and

(3➡) _ _ _ _ _ leave for

(4⬇) _ _ _ _ _ _ Claus

on Christmas (6➡) _ _ _?

Answer

(2⬇) _ _ _ _ _ _ _ _ _

and milk!

Word Bank

Santa	sleigh	quackers	snack
tree	ducks	Eve	cows

LEAPING LEPRECHAUNS

Name_____

Use words from the Word Bank to finish the riddle. Then use the same words to complete the puzzle.

Question

What did the

①⬇ _ _ _ _ _ _ _ _ _ _ _ _

do ⑤➡ _ _ _ _ he

stubbed his ②➡ _ _ _?

Answer

He called a toe-

③⬇ _ _ _ _ _

to take him to the

④➡ _ _ _ _ _ _ _.

Word Bank

truck   doctor   clover   leprechaun

green   shamrock   when   toe

"HARE'S" TO YOU!

Name_____

Use words from the
Word Bank to finish
the riddle. Then use
the same words to
complete the puzzle.

Question

Which Easter song is the

②⬇ __ __ __ __ __ __ __ __

of all

③➡ __ __ __ __ __ __ __ __ ?

Answer

④➡ __ __ __ __ __ comes

⑤➡ __ __ __ __ __ __

Cottontail,

①⬇ __ __ __ __ __ __ __ __

down the bunny trail.

Word Bank

Peter	hopping	singing	hare
Easter	eggs	favorite	rabbits

BUNNY TALES

Use words from the Word Bank to finish the riddle. Then use the same words to complete the puzzle.

Question

How do

①⬇ __ __ __ __ __ __

like to ②➡ __ __ __

their ⑤➡ __ __ __ __ ?

Answer

④➡ __ __ __ __ __ -

③⬇ __ __ __ __ __ up!

Word Bank

eggs	tail	bunny	eat
basket	rabbits	color	side

SCHOOL'S OUT!

Name_____

Use words from the Word Bank to finish the riddle. Then use the same words to complete the puzzle.

Question

Why is

①➡ ___ ___ ___ ___ ___ ___

out at three

②⬇ ___'___ ___ ___ ___ ___ ___?

Answer

Because the bell strikes one,

⑤➡ ___ ___ ___ ___ ___ ___ ___

two, strikes three — and

④➡ ___ ___ ___ are

③⬇ ___ ___ ___ ___!

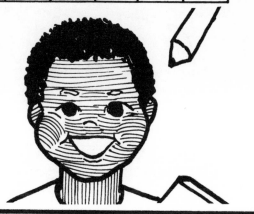

Word Bank

strikes	our	school	o'clock
pencil	out	you	grade

Noun Search

Name _____

Find the noun in each sentence.

Across
3. The chocolate cookies are crumbly.
5. The princess went shopping.

Down
1. Tip the box over.
2. We are sitting on the bicycle.
4. They were going to paint the building.
5. Watch the pony trot.
6. Getting the extra cupcake in was not easy.
7. I almost lost my skates.

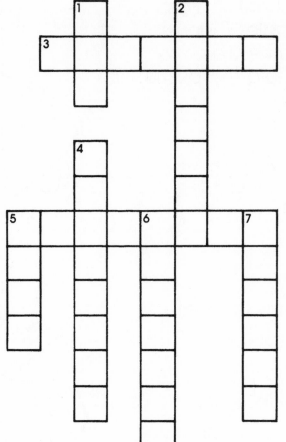

Word Bank

trot	cookies	cupcake	princess
bicycle	pony	building	getting
paint	box	skates	almost
shopping	tip	sitting	crumbly

Verb Search

Name _____

Find the verb in each sentence.

Across
2. The coyote howled at the moon.
4. My sister laughs at my jokes.
5. My friend visits me on the weekend.
7. A mule kicks with the hind legs.

Down
1. My mom works in a grocery store.
3. Mr. Jones drives our school bus.
4. The horses live in the stable.
6. He always trips over his shoe laces.

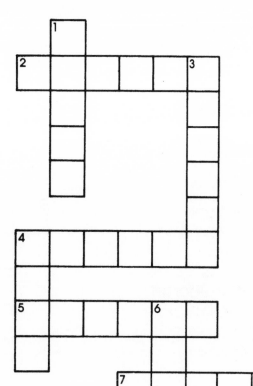

Word Bank

coyote	howled	horses	kicks
sister	mule	drives	store
visits	works	friend	trips
live	school	laces	laughs

Proper Shoppers

Name _____

Change these proper nouns to common nouns.

Across
2. Ford, Chevrolet, Toyota
5. Christmas or Halloween
7. California
8. Park Place, Lane Avenue, Willow Blvd.

Down
1. Abe Lincoln, George Washington, Ronald Reagan
3. Wednesday or Saturday
4. Africa, Asia, North America
6. Atlantic, Pacific, Arctic, Indian

Word Bank

continents	oceans	holiday	day
presidents	streets	state	cars

52

Punctuation Puffins

Name _____

Across

2. A question mark **(?)** is used with sentences that _____.
4. Commas **(,)** are _____.
7. An apostrophe **(')** in a contraction shows that a letter has been left _____.
8. Quotation marks **(" ")** are placed around what someone _____.

Down

1. Hyphens **(-)** are similar to _____.
3. A period **(.)** comes at the end of a _____.
5. Exclamation points **(!)** show _____.
6. A colon **(:)** is used before a _____ of things.

Word Bank

ask	statement	dashes	pauses
out	surprise	list	says

A Zoo for Two

Name _____

Find the 2-syllable words.

Across
2. horse–catfish–antelope
3. rabbit–ape–hare
4. elephant–otter–pelican
7. hippopotamus–quail–walrus

Down
1. kitten–dog–lamb
3. kangaroo–ant–raccoon
5. hummingbird–eagle–frog
6. rhinoceros–sheep–cougar

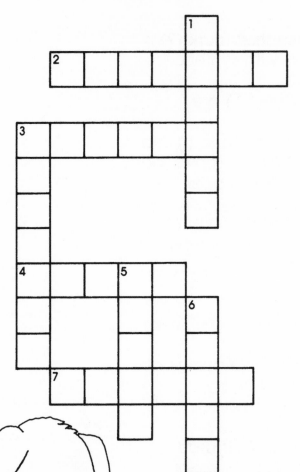

Word Bank

elephant	cougar	catfish	rhinoceros
rabbit	hare	raccoon	hummingbird
frog	otter	walrus	antelope
kitten	lamb	eagle	pelican

Contraction Actions

Name _____

Write the words which form the contractions.

Across
- 2. She's not home right now.
- 3. He'd like to go to the game.
- 5. They're all gone!
- 7. He's my best friend.

Down
- 1. I'll go get the pizza.
- 4. My friend doesn't live next door any more.
- 5. They've moved three times.
- 6. You've never been to the zoo.

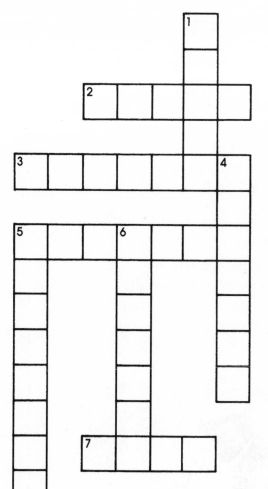

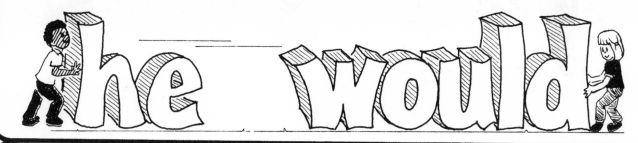

Word Bank

they have	they are	does not	he would
she is	I will	he is	you have

Ordinals, Ordinals

Name _____

Write the ordinals.

Across
2. before second
3. three before thirteenth
7. two after ninth
8. between second and fourth

Down
1. eight before fourteenth
4. four after sixteenth
5. nine before thirteenth
6. between first and third

Word Bank

tenth	twentieth	seventeenth	sixth
seventh	twelfth	thirteenth	eighth
fourth	fifth	eleventh	third
first	second	ninth	fourteenth

Shapes

Name _____

What is the shape?

across :

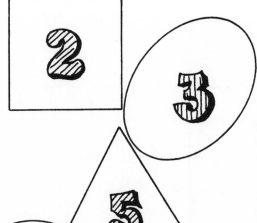

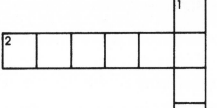
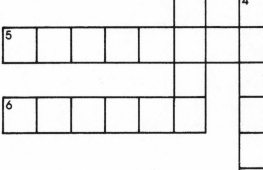
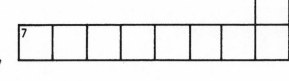

down :

Word Bank

oval	square	octagon	sphere
circle	rectangle	pentagon	pyramid
triangle	cone	hexagon	parallelogram
cylinder	cube	prism	

For Good Measure

Name _____

What is the measurement term?

Across
2. degrees in the metric system
6. There are 16 in one pound.
7. There are 12 in one foot.
8. 3 feet make 1 of these.

Down
1. metric liquid measurement
3. Twelve inches make one.
4. 100 of them make a meter.
5. There are 2 in one quart.

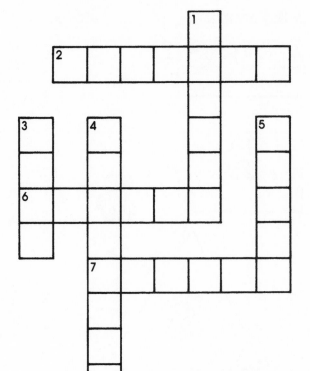

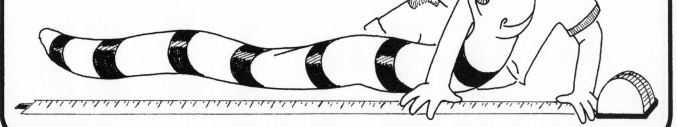

Word Bank

inches	pints	ounces	foot
yard	liters	centimeters	kilograms
degrees	grams	meter	ton
quarts	pounds	Celsius	

Just In Time

Name _____

Across

2. February is the only _____ with 28 days.
5. 10 years
7. 60 seconds make 1 _____.

Down

1. a celebration of 100 years
3. 365 days equal 1 _____.
4. 100 years
6. There are 52 in a year.

Word Bank

year	centennial	minute
weeks	decade	half-hour
century	month	day

Math Fun

Name _____

Across

2. In 6 + 7 = 13, the 6 and 7 are the _____.
4. 8 + 7 = 15 is an _____.
6. a part of a whole

Down

1. to put numbers together, as 7 + 9 = 16
3. guessing how many there are
5. In 16 ÷ 8 = 2, 2 is called the _____.
6. In 5 x 6 = 30, the 5 or 6 is called a _____.
7. the outside surface of something

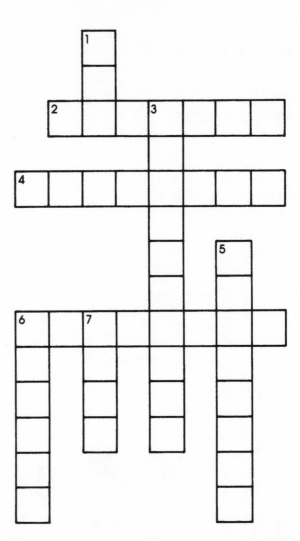

Word Bank

add	equation	perimeter	addends
sum	quotient	fraction	multiply
area	subtract	factor	estimating
times			

Did You Brush?

Name _____

Across
3. the back, grinding teeth
5. added to water and toothpaste to help prevent decay
7. the inner part of the tooth containing the nerves
8. His tooth hurt or _____.

Down
1. the place where teeth are anchored by the roots
2. invisible, sticky material on your teeth which causes decay
4. double-pointed tooth that tears food
5. a string used to clean between the teeth
6. hard, white outer surface of teeth

Word Bank

dentist	brush	cuspid	gums
root	plaque	bicuspid	molars
ached	drill	paste	pulp
fluoride	enamel	hygienist	floss

Trees and Leaves

Name _____

How well do you know your trees?

Across
2. the home of acorns
4. has nuts that are delicious when roasted
5. huge trees found in California

Down
1. The leaf of this tree is Canada's national symbol.
3. an evergreen tree
4. has red wood that is used to make chests for storing linens
6. a hardwood shade tree
7. has long, graceful branches that often touch the ground

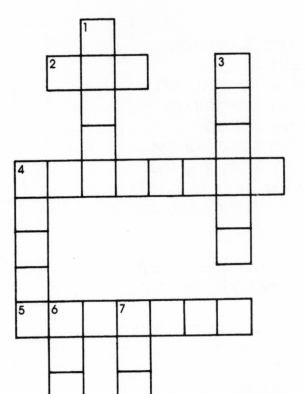

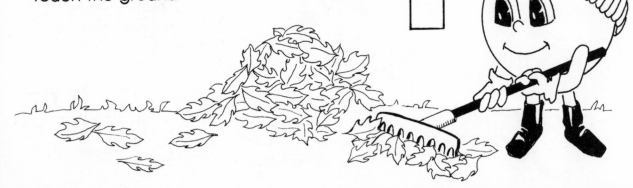

Word Bank

oak	spruce	locust	chestnut
cedar	pine	hemlock	willow
poplar	maple	redwood	dogwood
fir	elm	laurel	cherry

Leaping Lizards!

Name _____

Across

2. In Tyrannosaurus Rex, the Rex means _____.
4. The "tri" in Triceratops means it has _____ horns.
6. Stegosaurus had sharp _____ on its tail.
7. Some dinosaurs had bills like a _____.

Down

1. The "saur" in dinosaur means _____.
3. Stegosaurus had hard, bony _____ on its back.
4. From Greek, the "dino" in dinosaur means _____.
5. There are no more dinosaurs; they are _____.

Word Bank

Pterodactyl	Triceratops	duck	lizard
Allosaurus	Trachodon	plates	three
Stegosaurus	dinosaur	spikes	king
Brontosaurus	terrible	extinct	

The Daily News

Name _____

Across

1. information about what has just happened
3. the person who edits the newspaper
5. the condition of the air from day to day
7. listings and page numbers of parts of the paper
8. advertisements

Down

2. baseball, football, soccer
4. a special interest story found in the newspaper
6. newspaper cartoons

Word Bank

news	feature	TV guide	editorial
business	weather	editor	weddings
advice	births	comics	ads
sports	entertainment	index	

64

Orbiting in Space

Name _____

Across

2. Earth's sister planet, surrounded by clouds
3. the path a planet travels around the sun
4. the planet closest to the sun
6. the "Red Planet"
7. the eighth planet from the sun

Down

1. the largest planet in the solar system
5. the seventh planet in the solar system

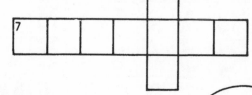

Word Bank

Earth	Venus	Mars	shuttle
Neptune	Jupiter	gravity	lunar
Pluto	Uranus	planet	solar
Saturn	Mercury	orbit	

The Noun Clown

Name_____

No clowning! You'll do well circling the 15 **nouns** in this wordsearch.

```
J U M P O L B O X R U N S
A C H I L D L C P U N T I
L X O S C U P C A K E U M
I L U M S K A T I N G R B
M S C H C L O W N O U T Z
O K S W I M M I N G R L O
K A I S L U C O O K I E S
H T F G I W H E N S L A L
I E O C B A S E B A L L T
B S D A R T I N G I H Z P
U T O O A B I C Y C L E R
I W A S R C L I M B E D I
L O C T Y F R I E N D S N
D L E A P E D C H O Z L C
I U B D E N T I S T K J E
N S T O O D U T G U L I S
G B R O K E N Y D O N E S
```

Word Bank

turtle	child	princess	clown	cookies
city	skates	baseball	cupcake	library
dentist	box	bicycle	friends	building

The Verb Van

Name_____

Get your wheels rolling!
Verbs are action words.
Circle the 15 **verbs** in
the wordsearch.

R	S	U	N	S	H	I	N	E	D	R	I	V	E	S	T
O	C	H	E	E	A	T	L	A	S	T	O	L	T	W	O
D	Y	O	W	H	O	L	B	L	N	R	A	N	O	A	H
E	B	W	C	I	X	I	T	A	H	C	M	A	R	L	O
L	F	L	E	W	E	V	I	U	N	K	K	I	C	K	U
R	N	E	P	O	N	I	N	G	K	R	A	F	H	S	S
D	O	D	L	B	E	N	C	H	R	A	C	E	D	B	E
I	W	T	U	S	N	G	O	S	M	A	R	T	I	U	L
V	I	S	I	T	S	F	A	H	E	L	M	V	W	B	G
I	E	A	B	S	U	D	T	I	R	E	V	A	O	L	J
N	O	L	W	N	A	P	H	L	I	O	N	W	R	U	K
G	U	V	B	J	U	M	P	I	N	G	T	M	K	E	K
T	H	I	S	T	L	E	G	L	N	A	W	D	S	I	S

Word Bank

laughs	drives	kick	howled	raced
flew	eat	walks	jumping	works
ran	rode	living	visits	diving

Plural Panda-Monium

Name_____

Circle the **plural forms** of these nouns.

A	L	O	B	T	P	A	N	D	A	R	T	L
S	O	Y	I	W	O	Z	W	O	M	E	N	C
C	X	T	M	I	C	E	B	C	A	M	O	L
N	E	S	R	T	I	G	H	B	T	K	M	E
T	N	W	R	C	E	E	L	B	C	E	N	A
U	L	R	Y	H	W	E	A	C	H	E	I	V
T	R	E	P	E	O	S	B	F	E	I	R	E
A	G	M	E	S	I	E	H	J	S	L	O	S
X	P	N	A	I	P	H	O	Y	B	S	K	A
E	N	S	C	H	I	L	D	R	E	N	O	B
S	T	E	H	W	P	C	I	V	B	G	E	J
W	A	C	E	H	T	O	H	D	E	E	R	C
P	B	U	S	E	S	S	A	H	P	W	X	L
E	O	R	T	S	U	D	L	Y	T	A	L	M
D	A	S	M	B	T	I	V	O	N	M	E	N
I	C	A	L	V	E	S	E	A	L	Y	C	A
X	O	T	R	G	I	C	S	G	U	O	N	P

Word Bank

man	child	ox	goose	peach
deer	calf	woman	bus	mouse
tax	match	leaf	half	witch

Here's the Pitch!

How many proper nouns can you catch? Each common noun in the word bank has a matching **proper noun** in the puzzle. Circle them with your favorite color.

Name_____

C	H	E	V	Y	L	D	K	O	R	T	C	H	D	F	M
I	S	G	N	O	P	A	C	I	F	I	C	L	A	U	A
B	C	M	B	N	A	V	Z	D	O	I	S	U	L	J	I
Y	E	O	W	L	V	I	O	G	D	T	M	P	L	Q	N
A	N	N	O	H	C	D	G	A	S	I	A	R	A	E	S
N	E	D	L	C	X	A	A	V	O	S	Y	R	S	O	T
K	I	A	V	R	E	A	G	A	N	B	F	M	C	P	R
E	B	Y	N	O	H	F	N	R	I	Y	C	L	O	T	E
E	Y	B	E	A	W	B	O	H	I	O	Z	A	W	D	E
S	M	C	I	N	D	Y	I	R	S	V	Y	N	B	L	T
N	I	M	K	R	I	A	J	A	X	I	C	M	O	G	A
S	I	H	A	L	L	O	W	E	E	N	M	R	Y	S	H
J	E	M	S	A	L	T	L	A	K	E	A	K	S	R	D

Word Bank

holiday	car	continent	girl	baseball team
lake	boy	president	street	football team
month	day	state	ocean	

Guide Word Giraffe

Name_____

Take a LONG look...
Circle only the words that would come between the guide words gape - grape in the dictionary.

N	T	G	A	S	O	L	G	I	B	R	T	G
A	X	L	S	G	U	E	S	S	G	E	T	A
Y	G	A	T	E	G	F	E	R	L	U	W	B
G	A	M	N	B	O	N	P	E	I	C	G	W
H	I	G	A	R	D	E	N	F	T	K	I	J
O	G	I	S	G	R	O	C	Y	T	G	A	O
K	I	G	B	G	I	L	L	S	E	R	N	F
A	R	Y	I	T	C	O	I	D	R	I	T	J
W	A	L	Y	B	E	C	G	A	L	T	M	I
N	F	E	A	G	I	G	G	L	E	S	H	G
E	F	R	G	T	O	H	H	Y	D	U	V	N
M	E	D	A	N	L	S	O	V	G	L	U	E
G	I	R	V	E	H	O	S	T	R	N	U	B
A	W	L	E	F	D	I	T	N	E	B	W	G
I	G	L	A	R	E	A	G	R	A	P	H	O
N	E	O	W	G	Y	I	M	A	S	O	T	T
P	L	I	W	L	G	R	A	I	N	O	L	K

Word Bank

gave	grain	glitter	guess	got
gas	grits	gab	giraffe	graph
get	giggle	garden	giant	ghost
glue	gain	glare	gate	gills

Punctuation Notation!

Name_____

"Tune in" on punctuation marks. Circle the names of 10 **punctuation marks** in this wordsearch. When do you use each mark?

Q	A	H	Y	P	H	E	N	N	Q	Z	C	T	U	V	H
U	U	Z	E	C	B	S	I	G	U	M	A	W	K	F	T
E	X	C	L	A	M	A	T	I	O	N	P	O	I	N	T
S	Q	S	I	P	O	R	E	J	T	D	X	E	D	U	F
T	U	P	D	O	B	F	P	L	A	Y	C	O	M	M	A
I	T	Q	Y	S	X	V	A	W	T	D	E	J	O	B	I
O	R	E	O	T	E	S	E	M	I	C	O	L	O	N	F
N	R	A	M	R	V	O	S	M	O	I	P	A	G	I	C
M	E	P	W	O	P	M	C	O	N	L	E	Z	G	E	K
A	C	A	N	P	K	O	I	R	M	Y	R	O	J	G	I
R	S	L	O	H	W	A	T	K	A	R	I	I	H	U	W
K	L	Q	U	E	M	O	N	E	R	H	O	V	M	U	L
R	C	O	L	O	N	L	B	S	K	N	D	A	S	H	A

Word Bank

period	dash	question mark	semi-colon
hyphen	colon	quotation mark	
comma	apostrophe	exclamation point	

Ssssyllable Sssssnakes! Name_____

"Ssss"earch for 15 snaky words that have **two** syllables.

F	E	S	J	U	N	G	L	E	O	V	G	N
C	U	A	D	N	P	O	O	D	E	I	M	O
O	S	T	Q	U	A	B	L	M	E	P	K	V
B	R	O	E	C	R	A	T	T	L	E	K	L
R	I	B	B	O	N	M	M	A	M	R	P	H
A	C	I	F	D	A	E	R	B	T	R	Z	A
E	O	V	M	A	S	P	O	T	T	E	D	R
H	A	R	M	F	U	L	C	N	O	P	E	M
F	H	I	S	S	I	N	G	J	K	T	S	L
V	I	G	K	N	A	Y	F	G	L	I	X	E
P	U	Q	L	E	Y	M	O	A	G	L	N	S
H	P	E	C	M	A	L	E	G	L	E	S	S
B	Y	U	L	O	D	T	O	A	S	M	C	H
P	T	A	E	M	I	C	K	R	E	Y	P	U
E	H	O	G	N	O	S	E	T	G	U	E	P
M	O	Y	E	R	E	K	T	E	H	Y	A	G
A	N	S	L	I	T	H	E	R	N	H	L	A

Word Bank

cobra	reptile	rattle	garter	spotted
python	jungle	legless	hognose	ribbon
hissing	harmless	viper	slither	harmful

Catching Contractions!

Find the **contractions** for the words in the word bank. You will have to add the missing apostrophes. Try to get a perfect score.

Name_____

Y	A	D	O	L	N	I	T	E	H	A	L	V	O	B	C
O	W	O	N	T	E	T	A	I	E	C	F	G	U	B	R
U	R	N	I	E	L	S	W	O	D	O	E	S	N	T	O
S	U	T	C	A	L	T	U	X	I	F	A	C	G	N	D
T	E	W	L	N	D	O	K	J	O	M	Y	S	C	B	I
T	H	E	Y	V	E	G	W	A	C	M	O	G	T	M	D
O	N	T	A	L	N	T	E	W	L	C	U	I	E	R	N
R	I	C	B	E	A	Y	N	D	O	N	R	K	E	W	T
N	H	R	E	I	S	N	T	N	C	K	E	O	G	R	E
W	L	G	E	L	I	Y	B	E	K	R	K	I	V	E	B
H	K	A	D	B	O	A	Z	N	E	G	I	L	M	S	A
O	L	T	H	E	Y	R	E	F	I	E	D	L	P	O	F
S	L	A	U	P	F	N	O	J	Y	O	U	V	E	R	T

Word Bank

did not	who is	they have	of the clock	is not
he would	does not	you have	do not	they are
it is	I will	will not	you are	I have

Ordinal Orchestra!

Name _____

Get with the beat! Ordinal numbers show order. Circle an **ordinal number** for each number in the word bank.

first
second
third

D	S	I	O	S	T	W	A	K	Y	R	O	U
U	I	N	S	I	X	T	E	E	N	T	H	D
W	X	H	E	T	L	H	E	I	N	W	I	F
N	T	D	V	G	O	I	C	G	T	E	A	O
E	H	C	E	O	N	R	C	H	A	N	N	U
N	B	R	N	I	D	T	U	T	N	T	E	R
I	A	R	T	H	W	E	A	H	M	I	M	T
N	U	T	H	S	R	E	W	I	K	E	S	H
T	A	S	C	H	O	N	T	O	S	T	E	K
H	F	J	K	Y	A	T	E	N	T	H	M	D
T	I	A	B	S	C	H	O	S	U	G	O	M
I	F	K	L	E	L	E	V	E	N	T	H	J
W	T	S	A	C	H	O	I	R	S	E	L	T
S	H	R	E	O	D	S	V	K	S	I	C	N
O	M	A	C	N	T	W	E	L	F	T	H	L
T	H	I	R	D	E	P	A	K	C	L	T	Y
P	G	E	N	R	C	A	H	F	I	R	S	T

Word Bank

example: 1 = first	4	7	10	13
2	5	8	11	16
3	6	9	12	20

Ship Shape!

Name_____

Ahoy, matey! Circle the names of the **geometric shapes** in the wordsearch. Can you draw the shapes?

P	O	C	U	B	E	W	S	N	H	B	A	L	R	G	O
A	O	Y	P	G	P	H	T	Y	E	S	P	R	I	S	M
R	I	L	C	R	S	E	R	T	X	R	E	M	S	P	O
A	M	I	P	E	A	H	I	S	A	I	N	E	F	H	G
L	Y	N	U	C	R	C	A	E	G	F	T	A	L	E	R
L	F	D	A	T	I	R	N	A	O	F	A	S	Y	R	O
E	L	E	O	A	K	A	G	N	N	E	G	B	I	E	S
L	C	R	B	N	A	M	L	O	I	C	O	N	E	W	O
O	C	T	A	G	O	N	E	S	U	L	N	M	C	D	V
G	T	I	G	L	N	G	N	C	I	R	C	L	E	L	A
R	S	U	A	E	M	I	T	O	S	N	S	M	U	B	L
A	W	V	C	E	S	K	E	P	Y	R	A	M	I	D	M
M	C	S	Q	U	A	R	E	H	M	I	S	U	T	B	Y

Word Bank

oval	circle	triangle	square	rectangle
cone	cylinder	octagon	pentagon	hexagon
cube	sphere	pyramid	parallelogram	prism

How do you measure up?

Name_____

The abbreviations in the word bank are for **measurement words.** Find those words in the wordsearch and circle in brown.

W	A	F	I	N	C	C	E	L	S	I	U	S
O	I	N	C	H	H	O	Z	I	D	L	A	R
P	S	V	M	G	R	A	M	T	O	D	M	C
O	T	I	E	H	L	A	R	E	D	I	B	E
U	C	E	T	V	Q	W	I	R	N	W	S	N
N	F	A	E	X	U	D	U	C	G	H	Y	T
D	E	C	R	H	A	P	U	C	A	P	E	I
H	A	J	Y	O	R	H	Y	N	L	G	O	M
I	G	P	N	O	T	O	C	W	L	O	L	E
K	I	L	O	G	R	A	M	E	O	T	X	T
Y	F	A	E	S	P	B	V	S	N	A	B	E
P	O	L	O	U	N	C	E	K	B	Q	U	R
E	O	P	V	I	F	Y	U	L	M	S	A	F
C	T	I	D	W	K	E	B	E	Y	A	R	D
V	H	O	S	P	I	N	T	C	A	Y	F	S
O	W	F	T	A	E	X	P	I	L	T	V	J
A	F	A	H	R	E	N	H	E	I	T	B	K

Word Bank

cm	in.	yd.	m	kg
C	ft.	lb.	F	l
g	pt.	qt.	gal.	oz.

76

Time's Up!

Name_____

Measuring time can make you "tick." Search for these "timely" answers in the puzzle.

E	C	T	O	D	W	A	B	Y	S	B	R	W	E	E	K
H	T	D	A	Y	B	M	O	E	A	I	L	W	P	N	A
A	E	F	Y	D	U	I	N	A	K	C	Y	G	J	I	H
L	C	I	L	R	E	N	S	R	L	E	A	L	N	I	A
F	L	M	G	O	F	U	T	I	B	N	P	O	Y	X	L
H	O	U	R	F	U	T	C	L	D	T	S	Z	R	O	F
O	D	P	I	L	C	E	W	T	C	E	O	P	U	J	M
U	L	S	W	K	I	C	L	C	E	N	T	U	R	Y	I
R	D	E	C	A	D	E	A	D	N	N	G	I	C	L	N
M	A	V	G	B	I	F	G	C	E	I	K	N	A	H	U
S	I	M	H	C	O	E	B	Y	E	A	R	W	E	P	T
V	M	O	N	T	H	K	O	R	G	L	N	A	P	G	E
O	S	M	A	C	Y	I	L	G	E	H	S	E	O	R	A

Word Bank

60 seconds = 1 _____   30 minutes = 1 _____

28-31 days = 1 _____   60 minutes = 1 _____

7 days = 1 _____   12 months = 1 _____

24 hours = 1 _____   10 years = 1 _____

100 years = 1 _____   200 years = 1 _____

30 seconds = 1 _____   365¼ days = 1 _____

"Term"-inal Math!

Name_____

Find these **math terms** in the puzzle. Be ready to tell what each term means.

$$6 \div 2 =$$

$$\begin{array}{r} 4 \\ \times 3 \\ \hline \end{array}$$

$$\begin{array}{r} 3 \\ -2 \\ \hline \end{array}$$

$$\begin{array}{r} 4 \\ +4 \\ \hline \end{array}$$

A	R	E	A	O	U	N	R	P	D	G	N	I
G	R	E	G	R	O	U	P	E	Q	S	U	M
F	U	M	P	V	I	S	N	R	O	A	P	E
R	A	D	D	E	N	D	Z	I	C	Q	N	E
A	D	I	T	O	A	N	G	M	K	U	J	S
C	U	F	A	C	T	O	R	E	U	O	T	T
T	I	F	P	O	L	S	W	T	B	T	V	I
I	G	E	L	N	H	Y	A	E	R	I	Q	M
O	C	R	M	G	I	M	G	R	U	E	D	A
N	A	E	T	R	C	M	B	V	I	N	F	T
A	S	N	B	U	K	E	F	I	F	T	O	I
M	I	C	S	E	G	T	O	D	E	N	I	N
G	U	E	R	N	I	R	C	B	Y	O	Z	G
P	N	E	O	T	L	Y	M	A	Z	O	P	R
U	M	Y	E	T	M	S	E	G	M	E	N	T
V	O	L	U	M	E	H	T	S	E	C	F	L
A	E	R	A	G	T	P	R	O	D	U	C	T

Word Bank

sum	product	factor	symmetry	quotient
addend	difference	fraction	estimating	area
congruent	volume	regroup	segment	perimeter

The "Brush-Off"!

"Brush up" on these **dental health words.** Mr. Tooth is "rooting" for you to find all 15 words.

Name_____

F	T	C	O	H	E	D	O	B	E	C	W	I	S	N	R
P	K	U	B	O	D	E	N	T	I	S	T	A	F	T	O
U	E	S	L	B	S	N	I	S	A	N	P	D	L	W	O
L	O	P	U	I	Z	T	K	F	L	O	S	S	U	I	T
P	P	I	L	C	D	I	F	Y	G	U	E	T	O	M	H
S	L	D	P	U	I	N	E	K	M	O	L	A	R	C	Y
A	A	L	V	S	H	U	B	L	A	K	R	Y	I	N	G
K	Q	P	S	P	I	E	N	A	M	E	L	L	D	M	I
P	U	O	C	I	A	N	E	C	M	G	I	A	E	B	E
K	E	B	W	D	U	I	N	C	I	S	O	R	S	R	N
Q	U	A	Z	H	C	B	U	K	Z	F	E	I	L	P	I
C	R	O	W	N	H	C	F	I	D	R	E	N	K	R	S
S	H	A	O	R	T	H	O	D	O	N	T	I	S	T	T

Word Bank

dentist	plaque	fluoride	cuspid	molar
crown	root	bicuspid	pulp	dentin
enamel	incisor	orthodontist	hygienist	floss

Trees...A Breeze!

Name_____

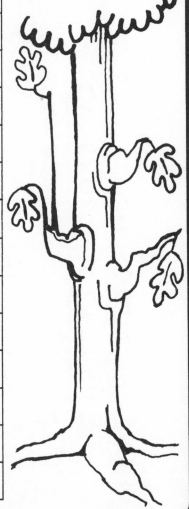

M	A	S	C	F	I	R	H	I	V	Y	E	O
M	D	Y	A	L	B	E	L	F	E	B	W	J
Q	U	C	E	D	A	R	Y	A	L	F	I	U
B	E	A	H	M	U	B	R	N	M	V	C	N
H	E	M	L	O	C	K	H	I	C	E	L	I
U	R	O	A	C	O	K	I	P	S	A	E	P
M	O	R	E	D	W	O	O	D	E	P	U	E
Y	L	E	I	C	M	A	I	S	L	P	L	R
P	O	R	L	O	C	U	S	T	U	O	D	A
W	I	L	L	O	W	I	R	M	X	P	D	O
S	P	I	C	R	U	E	R	T	P	L	O	D
O	D	L	A	R	P	I	N	E	G	A	U	F
A	W	A	M	R	O	T	C	U	Y	R	G	I
K	O	U	C	P	E	S	P	R	U	C	E	D
X	E	R	B	F	T	A	C	E	S	B	V	Q
C	H	E	S	T	N	U	T	H	I	A	C	S
N	O	L	M	A	I	T	O	M	A	P	L	E

Word Bank

elm	oak	sycamore	laurel
willow	pine	chestnut	juniper
poplar	spruce	locust	redwood
fir	maple	hemlock	cedar

The Space Place!

Name_____

"Blast-off" into this space wordsearch. "Launch" your mind to find 15 **space words.** Can you define them?

R	C	O	S	T	A	R	S	F	I	C	A	N	C	G	O
E	F	S	L	I	W	U	A	N	K	U	T	L	O	S	P
V	K	I	A	U	R	O	T	L	P	N	M	O	N	H	S
O	R	M	U	C	O	M	E	T	S	I	O	F	S	U	Z
L	T	U	N	W	A	K	L	G	E	V	S	H	T	T	O
V	P	R	C	X	I	E	L	H	C	E	P	D	E	T	C
E	P	O	H	A	C	L	I	S	O	R	H	E	L	L	B
K	U	T	A	V	D	L	T	I	B	S	E	G	L	E	G
G	R	A	V	I	T	Y	E	H	K	E	R	N	A	M	A
A	W	T	G	S	P	A	C	E	C	B	E	L	T	V	L
N	B	I	M	C	A	P	S	U	L	E	A	K	I	S	A
R	E	N	Y	A	R	M	S	K	I	R	E	T	O	E	X
B	Y	G	R	A	S	T	R	O	N	A	U	T	N	N	Y

Word Bank

shuttle	rotating	satellite	universe	constellation
stars	astronaut	galaxy	gravity	capsule
comets	atmosphere	revolve	launch	space

Dynamite Dinosaurs!

Name _____

```
L W D A O T R S E C A Y L
T R I C E R A T O P S G B
Y O P F S A R E G T C U R
R P L I A C F G O E S D O
A V O G E H V O E R D W N
N E D U P O B S I O C M T
N U O A S D K A R D F I O
O I C N L O S U W A D N S
S G U O P N A R J C E P A
A Y S D M E C U W T H E U
U A L O R J V S K Y V O R
R B E N U S R C I L U N U
U S V P S J M I A N L O S
S O A L L O S A U R U S Y
C G T E L A L C B W U V D
B R A C H I O S A U R U S
A F I K N A Y U G H O Q A
```

Word Bank

Triceratops   Stegosaurus   Tyrannosaurus   Diplodocus

Brachiosaurus   Trachodon   Brontosaurus

Allosaurus   Iguanodon   Pterodactyl

    82

Extra! Extra!
Read All About It!

Name_____

These **newspaper words** are "hot off the press." Circle them and then find them in your newspaper.

B	I	F	L	C	O	M	I	C	S	B	W	C
S	A	N	W	L	A	D	V	I	C	E	E	S
P	M	F	E	A	T	U	R	E	S	H	A	P
O	H	B	A	S	R	E	L	X	P	S	T	O
R	N	U	B	S	O	S	B	I	R	T	H	S
T	D	S	V	I	E	I	F	A	P	R	E	O
S	T	I	U	F	B	G	C	D	A	N	R	I
C	V	N	M	I	E	A	L	E	R	Y	P	N
E	G	E	H	E	L	P	W	A	N	T	E	D
L	U	S	Q	D	O	U	L	T	I	G	Y	E
P	I	S	K	A	H	J	E	H	S	C	T	X
A	D	R	E	D	H	W	O	S	R	E	V	I
W	E	L	I	S	O	X	B	O	S	L	A	N
E	N	T	E	R	T	A	I	N	M	E	N	T
P	I	A	T	F	C	Y	O	W	N	D	O	B
J	A	H	E	D	I	T	O	R	I	A	L	N
W	E	D	D	I	N	G	S	G	E	N	S	O

Word Bank

comics	classified ads	tv guide	index	births
sports	editorial	help wanted	business	advice
weather	entertainment	weddings	features	deaths

All Systems Go!

Name_____

Our solar system has nine planets. Circle their names in blue. Circle the other "astro" words in yellow.

V	I	T	A	E	A	R	T	H	C	U	L	P	H	E	Z
E	C	M	I	C	R	A	S	I	L	S	A	N	V	J	K
U	R	A	N	U	S	O	H	M	Q	U	V	E	N	U	S
M	A	O	D	C	U	Y	H	O	R	L	D	P	C	I	A
E	T	M	S	L	V	I	B	O	L	U	E	T	G	B	T
M	E	R	C	U	R	Y	S	N	J	N	M	U	N	T	U
P	R	E	Y	A	R	Y	T	S	O	A	M	N	D	A	R
T	S	M	E	J	U	P	I	T	E	R	Y	E	L	U	N
F	U	R	A	E	Y	L	G	I	O	V	Y	M	F	S	A
C	O	R	B	I	T	U	B	I	K	P	L	A	N	E	T
M	V	A	F	C	R	T	O	L	K	N	C	I	D	W	N
B	P	E	Y	S	S	O	L	A	R	M	K	A	P	O	S
M	A	R	S	L	N	E	V	A	C	R	E	J	H	O	M

Word Bank

planet	orbit	moons	craters	Neptune
Mercury	Mars	Earth	Pluto	Venus
Jupiter	Saturn	Uranus	lunar	solar

It's Your Serve!

Circle the sport in which each piece of equipment is used.

O	B	A	S	K	E	T	B	A	L	L	S	M	P	S	A
J	R	M	K	I	H	O	P	S	C	O	T	C	H	A	R
B	O	S	I	W	O	C	H	L	I	T	E	N	N	I	S
A	C	P	I	N	G	P	O	N	G	K	R	S	V	E	N
S	B	R	N	T	S	K	A	T	I	N	G	A	L	B	E
E	I	F	G	C	W	L	E	A	V	K	O	N	G	O	X
B	A	C	V	F	O	O	T	B	A	L	L	W	O	X	A
A	S	R	I	N	G	T	O	S	S	R	A	D	L	I	E
L	Y	N	U	K	L	H	O	C	K	E	Y	F	F	N	O
L	T	I	K	N	G	A	O	L	P	U	C	T	O	G	I
B	H	O	R	S	E	B	A	C	K	R	I	D	I	N	G
G	Y	M	N	A	S	T	I	C	S	E	B	N	D	O	W
K	D	S	W	I	M	M	I	N	G	C	E	L	A	O	S

Word Bank

racquet	bat & ball	helmet	basket	puck
skis	large gloves	saddle	paddle	stone
tees	skates	balance beam	goggles	ring

Dictionary Diploma!

Name _____

Across
1. Part of a word
3. A mini-dictionary in the back of a school text
7. The syllable that is stressed in a word
8. All dictionaries have pronunciation _____.

Down
1. To pronounce a word
2. The word you are looking up
3. Words at the top of a dictionary page that help you find the entry word quickly
4. A noun, verb, or adverb is called a part of _____.
5. To tell the meaning of a word
6. To give more force to a syllable

Word Bank

keys	stress	guide words	respellings
entry	syllable	pronunciation	accent
glossary	inflection	word history	speech
say	schwa	define	

What's In a Name?

Name _____

Across
1. March is named for this Roman god of war.
3. January is named for this god of gates and doors.
5. October's origin – the Roman number 8
7. Wednesday is named for this Roman god.

Down
1. Monday's origin – the ___ ___ ___ ___'s day.
2. Sunday is named for the center of our solar system.
4. Saturday is named for this Roman god of agriculture.
6. Thursday is named for this god of thunder and lightning.

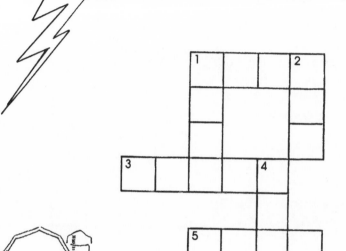

Word Bank

Frigga	Decem	Augustus	Februa
Tiu	Octo	Junius	Julius
Moon	Sun	Janus	Caesar
Thor	Mai	Mars	Woden
Saturn	Aprilis	Septem	Novem

Health Helpers!

Name _____

Across

2. You need _____ to work and play.
4. Nutrient necessary for growth and good health
6. Nutrient which stores energy
7. Plants that are used as a source of food
9. Wheat, corn, rice, and oats are examples of these.
10. Foods made from milk – they are a source of calcium.
11. Your body at rest

Down

1. Steak, liver, lamb – these are good sources of iron.
3. About 60% of your body is _____.
5. A nutrient needed for many jobs, including building strong bones and teeth
8. To make your body work

Word Bank

exercise	vitamins	meat	energy
diet	minerals	vegetables	rest
fats	water	fruit	cleanliness
proteins	dairy	grains	sleep

88

Don't Pollute!

Name _____

Across

1. The wearing away of the earth by wind, water, and ice
6. This type of accident endangers ocean life.
8. The science of the relationship between living things and their environment
10. The natural, living part of our world

Down

2. Energy which is sent out from atoms and molecules as they undergo change
3. Smoke and fog
4. This makes our environment dirty and unhealthy.
5. To use something over and over again
7. Chemicals used to control insects – they can harm plant and animal life.
9. Trash thrown about and not disposed of

Word Bank

smog	pollution	recycle	reservoir
exhaust	pesticides	litter	landfill
sanitation	conservation	environment	ecology
radiation	erosion	incinerator	oil spill

Land and Water

Name _____

Across

4. One of the seven large bodies of land on the earth
8. The deep, narrow part of a waterway
9. An inland body of water
10. A great body of salt water

Down

1. High, rocky land – it usually has steep sides and a pointed or rounded top.
2. A land area with very little water or plant-life
3. A body of land almost surrounded by water
5. A large stream of water which empties into an ocean or lake
6. A level area of land found in the mountains
7. A body of land which is totally surrounded by water

Word Bank

plateau	gulf	ocean	river
desert	island	peninsula	sea
canal	lake	continent	strait
channel	mountain	delta	tributary

Ocean Going

Name _____

Across

2. A large area of water which extends from the ocean into the coastline
5. Its clusters of tentacles resemble flowers.
6. A large ocean which meets the western coast of the United States
9. An animal with five or more arms resembling a star
10. Ocean plant-life

Down

1. The flow of water in the ocean
3. The ocean located between North America and Europe
4. A person who studies ocean life
7. A six-foot unit used for measuring water depth
8. A small fish that resembles a horse

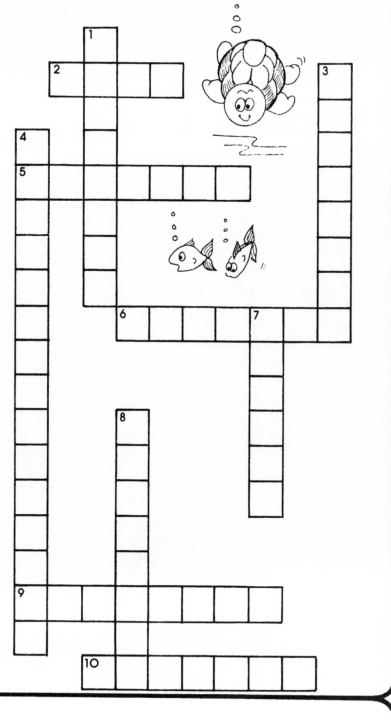

Word Bank

Atlantic	Pacific	Indian	Arctic
Antarctic	currents	oceanography	continent
coral reef	seaweed	tidal wave	anemone
sea horse	sea urchin	starfish	plankton
gulf	fathom	sonar	marine biologist

91

Star-Struck

Name _____

Across

1. Any object that orbits another object
4. Everything that exists
6. The path of a planet around the sun
9. The sun and all the heavenly bodies that revolve around it

Down

2. An instrument used for observing objects that are far away
3. A group of stars named after an object they resemble
5. The study of stars and planets
7. A reuseable spacecraft
8. A grouping of millions of stars

Word Bank

atmosphere	telescope	astronomy	universe
planetarium	satellite	constellation	orbit
astrology	gravity	asteroid	galaxy
meteor	observatory	solar system	shuttle

Hot Off the Press!

Name _____

Across

1. A person who reports the news
5. A major story in the newspaper
8. To prepare and sell a newspaper
9. A listing of the contents of a newspaper
10. Cartoons found in the newspaper

Down

2. An article which expresses the opinion of a newspaper's editor
3. This section tells us if we will need an umbrella.
4. The top, front page title of a newspaper story
6. An agreement to receive and pay for the newspaper on a regular basis
7. The section which tells who won last night's basketball game

Word Bank

index	headline	masthead	lead
editorial	feature	comics	weather
classified ads	subscription	publish	help wanted
sports	entertainment	column	reporter

Forests

Name _____

Across
3. Making the best use of and protecting the forests, land, and other natural resources
5. A mixture of ground up wood used for making paper
6. Layers of wood glued and pressed together
8. A place where trees are grown for harvesting
9. A substance put into the soil to give extra food to plants

Down
1. A person who is employed to guard the forest
2. A pond of water near a sawmill that is used for storing logs
4. A place where logs are sawed into boards
7. A lumberjack
8. A region near the Equator with rain forests

Word Bank

evergreens	fertilizer	forest ranger	logger
machete	conservation	millpond	national forest
plywood	pulp	rain forest	sawmill
tree farm	tropical	water cycle	watershed

Scary, Scary, Dictionary

Using the dictionary does not have to be scary! Find these words in the puzzle.

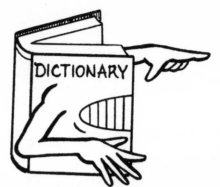

Name _____

C	T	H	E	A	C	C	E	N	T	Y	S	I	K	B	U	G	A	N	S	C	T
B	I	F	Y	O	S	C	H	W	A	R	N	E	D	P	V	E	N	T	R	Y	D
D	L	B	C	E	H	F	I	H	C	S	O	R	O	R	B	T	A	S	W	H	I
I	L	K	G	U	I	D	E	W	O	R	D	S	L	O	I	O	D	W	I	M	A
F	U	R	L	A	T	M	G	I	E	N	T	E	P	N	S	P	E	L	N	T	C
B	S	G	O	S	U	C	D	P	I	D	W	P	J	U	C	S	F	A	F	H	R
M	T	O	S	Y	L	L	A	B	L	E	S	D	L	N	N	D	I	Z	L	P	I
K	R	B	S	P	A	R	T	O	F	S	P	E	E	C	H	W	N	M	E	M	T
J	A	C	A	M	T	L	A	B	W	G	Y	X	L	I	R	S	I	S	C	W	I
O	T	H	R	Y	H	I	C	E	R	L	D	R	A	A	P	L	T	L	T	A	C
A	I	L	Y	I	L	N	W	S	C	H	P	A	C	T	E	R	I	K	I	T	A
W	O	R	D	H	I	S	T	O	R	Y	C	R	O	I	M	P	O	C	O	E	L
B	N	T	Y	H	R	E	A	N	Y	A	E	N	S	O	J	L	N	A	N	R	M
E	F	I	S	O	F	A	O	L	N	K	P	R	B	N	D	T	S	E	S	N	A
L	A	E	G	N	I	R	E	S	P	E	L	L	I	N	G	S	Y	R	O	I	R
O	S	W	A	P	R	S	M	K	T	O	I	R	W	C	D	E	S	A	L	E	K

Word Bank

entry	illustration	guide words	pronunciation
accent	schwa	syllables	word history
respellings	definitions	inflections	part of speech
diacritical mark	glossary		

Call It a Day!

Name _____

A	B	R	S	A	T	U	R	D	A	Y	F	A	H	R	D
M	G	O	U	D	H	P	I	O	G	A	R	J	L	P	O
O	S	B	N	O	V	E	M	B	E	R	E	T	U	D	R
N	O	I	D	H	A	S	P	A	B	L	O	C	R	N	O
D	M	Y	A	G	I	R	M	G	T	A	S	P	E	I	E
A	P	L	Y	N	S	F	E	B	R	U	A	R	Y	T	O
Y	G	O	S	C	A	U	W	H	K	O	L	T	M	O	X
C	O	S	H	J	I	A	C	A	R	B	R	U	B	C	M
S	D	E	T	H	U	R	S	D	A	Y	J	E	M	T	S
I	E	T	C	E	H	L	O	N	L	I	C	S	A	O	E
L	C	A	N	Y	W	H	Y	L	F	E	B	D	N	B	P
F	E	N	D	C	O	M	A	M	O	R	I	A	H	E	T
E	M	U	O	R	U	S	I	A	J	U	G	Y	S	R	E
F	B	I	M	I	L	A	P	R	I	L	M	S	H	N	M
O	E	R	Z	A	G	T	O	C	S	C	I	T	H	E	B
F	R	I	D	A	Y	R	O	H	X	Y	T	H	I	R	E
L	O	T	E	F	O	W	D	C	I	K	O	W	E	S	R
H	E	W	E	D	N	E	S	D	A	Y	J	L	I	M	A
F	O	E	G	I	Y	W	R	A	U	G	U	S	T	A	L
I	N	L	O	F	J	A	N	U	A	R	Y	C	I	Z	R

The names of the days and the months come from the origins listed in the Clue Bank. Match each word origin with the right name. Then find the names in the puzzle.

Clue Bank

Decem	Mars	Septem	Junius Family
Janus	Sun	Saturn	Julius Caesar
Moon	Maia	Februa	Thor's Day
Woden	Aprilis	Octem	Augustus Caesar
Frigga	Tiu	Novem	

Healthy and Happy!

Name _____

G	I	E	A	E	N	O	F	R	U	I	T	E	Y	M	T
P	R	O	T	E	I	N	S	V	H	E	V	A	U	I	Z
E	S	T	O	B	F	S	O	S	L	E	E	P	X	L	Y
R	E	R	H	I	O	R	L	E	B	A	D	C	B	K	N
R	N	D	H	O	E	E	W	M	T	O	R	B	W	P	O
O	E	E	N	V	I	T	A	M	I	N	S	F	D	R	A
F	R	O	L	R	B	E	T	E	I	V	A	E	V	O	U
S	G	A	I	C	E	R	E	A	L	N	V	G	N	D	D
U	Y	E	A	U	G	U	R	S	T	Y	E	A	U	U	I
F	E	R	K	E	H	T	E	T	W	E	G	H	I	C	E
S	A	S	R	T	O	N	S	G	A	T	E	U	M	T	T
C	Y	T	L	W	E	I	S	H	U	R	T	I	I	S	I
M	S	O	S	T	A	R	C	H	I	L	A	T	N	T	R
K	R	S	E	I	L	H	I	E	T	Y	B	J	E	O	K
E	P	M	E	A	T	O	R	I	A	I	L	I	R	S	U
I	Y	E	A	M	E	N	D	T	O	U	E	K	A	R	N
O	R	W	T	T	H	E	O	N	E	W	S	C	L	T	O
N	A	F	E	X	E	R	C	I	S	E	H	A	S	B	A
C	L	E	A	N	L	I	N	E	S	S	U	I	O	Q	O
U	O	H	N	H	G	O	Y	A	G	R	I	N	E	P	R
C	T	E	Y	C	U	Y	G	R	A	I	N	L	A	F	L

To stay healthy, you need food, exercise, and rest. Find 17 words that are necessary for good health.

Word Bank

exercise	diet	fats	proteins
vitamins	minerals	water	milk products
meat	vegetables	fruit	grain
cereal	starch	energy	cleanliness
sleep			

Pollution Is a Dirty Word!

Name _____

Help clean up our planet by finding out about these ecology words. Circle each word in the puzzle after you know its meaning.

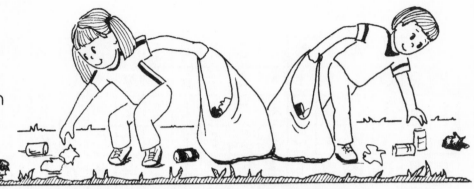

A	T	D	R	A	D	I	A	T	I	O	N	Y	E	C	R	O	C	A	R	O	N
L	O	P	M	E	V	I	X	B	A	S	L	K	O	E	X	H	A	U	S	T	P
A	H	O	O	L	E	H	C	N	I	S	R	T	C	L	O	E	Y	P	A	L	A
N	E	L	I	T	T	E	R	B	U	G	C	A	L	O	G	N	E	U	N	M	E
D	S	L	L	D	A	I	B	Y	N	E	K	E	A	S	R	V	B	L	I	N	R
F	M	U	S	O	R	K	P	R	E	C	Y	C	L	E	O	I	M	V	T	B	O
I	O	T	P	A	T	C	E	N	H	I	E	O	A	D	L	R	E	W	A	T	S
L	R	I	I	F	L	I	S	E	O	M	U	L	T	E	I	O	Y	V	T	C	I
L	D	O	L	U	K	N	T	A	B	I	L	O	O	X	B	N	P	U	I	D	O
N	T	N	L	O	N	T	I	K	E	S	O	G	A	E	O	M	E	G	O	I	N
V	B	O	S	T	R	S	C	I	Y	L	S	Y	W	A	L	E	K	C	N	B	A
R	E	S	E	R	V	O	I	R	M	J	O	L	P	F	F	N	E	S	N	A	T
Y	S	E	R	T	R	A	D	E	P	I	L	T	A	E	N	T	M	E	Y	A	R
L	E	M	C	O	N	S	E	R	V	A	T	I	O	N	Y	D	O	P	O	R	A
G	O	E	V	I	W	K	S	Y	K	S	I	O	N	A	P	L	S	M	O	G	E
P	I	N	C	I	N	E	R	A	T	O	R	L	I	M	O	B	J	K	T	K	M

Word Bank

smog	pollution	recycle	reservoir
exhaust	pesticides	litterbug	landfill
sanitation	conservation	environment	ecology
radiation	erosion	incinerator	oil spills

Gateway for Geography

Name _____

16 geographical words are hidden in this puzzle. Circle them. Then be ready to explain each one.

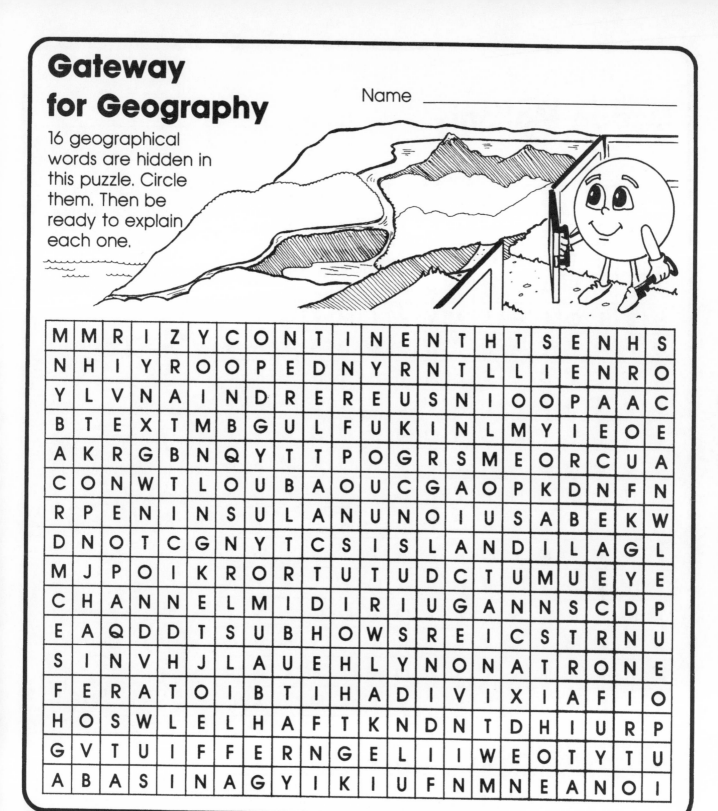

M	M	R	I	Z	Y	C	O	N	T	I	N	E	N	T	H	T	S	E	N	H	S
N	H	I	Y	R	O	O	P	E	D	N	Y	R	N	T	L	L	I	E	N	R	O
Y	L	V	N	A	I	N	D	R	E	R	E	U	S	N	I	O	O	P	A	A	C
B	T	E	X	T	M	B	G	U	L	F	U	K	I	N	L	M	Y	I	E	O	E
A	K	R	G	B	N	Q	Y	T	T	P	O	G	R	S	M	E	O	R	C	U	A
C	O	N	W	T	L	O	U	B	A	O	U	C	G	A	O	P	K	D	N	F	N
R	P	E	N	I	N	S	U	L	A	N	U	N	O	I	U	S	A	B	E	K	W
D	N	O	T	C	G	N	Y	T	C	S	I	S	L	A	N	D	I	L	A	G	L
M	J	P	O	I	K	R	O	R	T	U	T	U	D	C	T	U	M	U	E	Y	E
C	H	A	N	N	E	L	M	I	D	I	R	I	U	G	A	N	N	S	C	D	P
E	A	Q	D	D	T	S	U	B	H	O	W	S	R	E	I	C	S	T	R	N	U
S	I	N	V	H	J	L	A	U	E	H	L	Y	N	O	N	A	T	R	O	N	E
F	E	R	A	T	O	I	B	T	I	H	A	D	I	V	I	X	I	A	F	I	O
H	O	S	W	L	E	L	H	A	F	T	K	N	D	N	T	D	H	I	U	R	P
G	V	T	U	I	F	F	E	R	N	G	E	L	I	I	W	E	O	T	Y	T	U
A	B	A	S	I	N	A	G	Y	I	K	I	U	F	N	M	N	E	A	N	O	I

Word Bank

basin	gulf	ocean	river
bay	island	peninsula	sea
canal	lake	continent	strait
channel	mountain	delta	tributary

Ocean Motion!

Name _____

B	A	C	F	S	E	A	U	R	C	H	I	N	U	M	C
S	E	O	G	E	I	N	A	X	I	N	D	I	A	N	O
E	A	N	T	A	R	C	T	I	C	P	E	O	N	I	R
A	F	T	U	W	L	C	S	R	N	T	G	C	E	S	A
H	B	I	O	E	G	I	A	V	P	I	M	E	O	T	L
O	P	N	V	E	A	L	T	W	O	D	E	A	S	A	R
R	U	E	I	D	E	T	L	A	M	A	K	N	I	R	E
S	R	N	D	A	P	L	A	V	E	L	S	O	F	F	E
E	S	T	L	V	L	C	N	O	R	W	D	G	R	I	F
Y	O	L	G	O	A	H	T	S	R	A	O	R	M	S	G
A	N	E	M	O	N	E	I	H	D	V	I	A	R	H	N
N	A	M	Y	E	K	B	C	F	L	E	S	P	T	X	E
P	R	I	T	N	T	O	H	P	A	X	Y	H	I	W	L
L	I	S	B	T	O	S	W	A	C	G	F	Y	V	V	N
A	M	A	R	I	N	E	B	I	O	L	O	G	I	S	T
R	E	K	M	Y	A	R	H	D	K	I	C	J	S	B	O
C	U	R	R	E	N	T	S	W	O	M	T	B	K	W	A
T	L	U	G	U	L	F	S	T	R	E	A	M	I	A	C
I	H	M	D	M	E	L	K	I	P	A	C	I	F	I	C
C	E	Y	N	S	F	A	T	H	O	M	S	C	E	R	Y

The ocean is in continuous motion. Dive into the "deep" to find these underwater words.

Word Bank

Atlantic	Pacific	Indian	Arctic
Antarctic	currents	oceanography	continent
coral reef	seaweed	tidal wave	anemone
seahorse	sea urchin	starfish	plankton
Gulf Stream	fathoms	sonar	marine biologist

Lost in Space

Name _____

These space words are "out of sight." Can you find them and bring them back? Find out what each one means.

C	I	M	Y	C	T	S	A	N	A	S	T	R	O	N	O	M	Y	E	D	K	Y
I	M	E	A	D	E	L	I	Q	R	U	P	E	R	O	K	E	L	S	R	C	T
X	E	N	T	O	L	O	S	I	M	I	L	O	B	A	S	R	G	N	I	O	L
F	T	E	M	F	E	U	O	D	B	A	A	Z	I	R	N	B	R	E	L	N	E
O	E	L	O	E	S	A	L	U	D	I	N	C	T	I	K	R	A	I	R	S	N
T	O	R	S	I	C	F	A	W	X	I	E	Y	B	G	A	H	V	O	S	T	S
E	R	M	P	E	O	S	R	B	E	R	T	G	B	A	B	T	I	B	G	E	J
Y	N	O	H	K	P	R	S	W	E	S	A	T	E	L	L	I	T	E	B	L	U
F	L	O	E	F	E	A	Y	I	T	N	R	E	S	A	R	O	A	I	H	L	F
V	E	B	R	I	F	U	S	D	A	S	I	U	L	X	O	B	T	E	X	A	S
O	B	S	E	R	V	A	T	O	R	Y	U	S	E	Y	A	G	I	R	G	T	F
S	W	I	A	V	T	S	E	G	A	V	M	O	L	S	T	E	O	D	A	I	K
B	L	F	E	H	O	I	M	J	N	I	Y	R	I	W	O	L	N	Y	S	O	U
I	A	S	T	R	O	L	O	G	Y	E	D	O	P	I	X	E	T	A	I	N	P
L	E	P	A	O	W	S	K	A	C	N	A	S	T	E	R	O	I	D	N	T	E
G	U	N	I	V	E	R	S	E	K	E	E	C	A	H	T	N	A	O	W	N	Y

Word Bank

atmosphere
planetarium
astrology
meteor

telescope
satellite
gravitation
observatory

astronomy
constellation
asteroid
solar system

universe
orbit
galaxy

Time for Measurement

It's time to learn about measurement. Measure your knowledge by seeing how long it takes you to find 21 measurement terms.

H	M	O	I	R	A	U	L	S	E	E	R	U	R	T	C	N	O	M	P	N	O
L	S	E	C	O	N	D	S	E	M	A	O	I	T	Y	A	R	T	F	Y	P	A
A	R	Y	U	R	N	M	A	B	R	C	S	U	O	D	E	I	O	Q	U	I	F
S	E	K	G	S	C	I	G	Y	S	T	O	N	E	O	C	A	A	E	T	N	R
V	M	I	D	L	G	I	A	S	O	L	B	T	Y	Q	U	A	R	T	U	T	E
M	I	L	E	E	T	F	I	O	G	A	T	G	R	I	S	L	C	D	M	B	E
D	M	O	O	S	I	S	L	S	A	L	A	H	E	L	P	S	Y	E	M	N	D
E	I	M	A	L	A	O	H	Y	L	Y	L	I	T	E	R	O	M	R	E	A	G
I	E	E	Y	O	F	A	C	O	L	Y	E	N	R	S	R	O	I	R	T	D	E
C	U	T	B	H	O	U	R	S	O	K	H	C	G	H	U	V	N	F	E	A	P
U	H	E	F	E	O	Y	C	U	N	H	M	H	A	M	G	O	U	A	R	N	O
P	D	R	A	T	T	R	U	I	I	W	T	B	I	G	A	E	T	Y	D	W	U
A	T	E	D	R	S	N	T	C	H	U	H	I	T	O	T	W	E	E	K	W	N
V	O	C	E	H	W	T	M	O	U	N	C	E	A	U	C	U	A	T	I	N	D
G	M	O	N	T	H	O	A	H	U	R	T	W	C	K	I	Y	S	A	N	N	O
E	O	R	A	E	W	H	T	N	T	I	S	S	Y	A	R	D	W	E	K	A	I

Word Bank

second	minute	hour	day
week	month	year	inch
foot	yard	mile	cup
pint	quart	gallon	ounce
pound	ton	meter	liter
kilometer			

Answer Key

Short a Attack

Name _____

Across
1. a small house, made from logs
4. a fire-breathing animal
5. the home of a king or queen
8. a red fruit

Down
2. a spaceman
3. the horn of a deer
6. a baby frog
7. the opposite of first

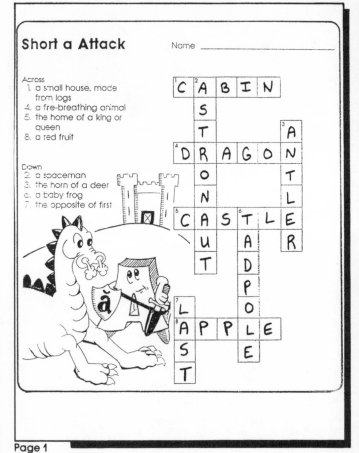

Crossword answers:
- 1 Across: CABIN
- 4 Across: DRAGON
- 5 Across: CASTLER
- Down: ASTRONAUT, ANTLER, TADPOLE
- 7 LAST
- APPLE

Swimming with Short i

Name _____

Across
2. a branch of a tree
3. the root word of missing
4. a sound made with your lips
6. a voyage or journey

Down
1. to leap or jump lightly
2. moving in water
4. the season following fall
5. narrow or skinny

Crossword answers:
- STICK / SKIP
- MISS
- SWIMMING
- WHISTLE / THIN
- WINTER
- TRIP

The Seven Short e's

Name _____

Across
2. the grade after first grade
5. something taken when you are sick
7. a movie about cowboys and Indians

Down
1. Food gives us _____
3. to make your body work
4. going down a hill on a sled
6. people or things you speak about

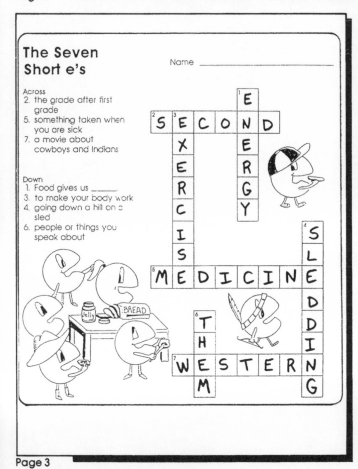

Crossword answers:
- SECOND
- ENERGY
- EXERCISE
- MEDICINE
- SLEDDING
- THEM
- WESTERN

The Short o Doctor

Name _____

Across
1. the first bird you see in spring
4. the person who makes you well when you are sick
5. to let something fall
7. a person who steals

Down
2. a baby's toy
3. a baby just learning to walk
6. when it's hard to see outside

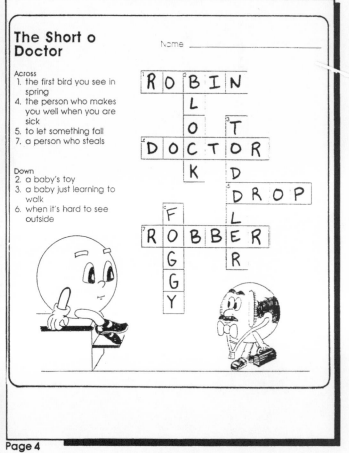

Crossword answers:
- ROBIN
- BLOCK
- TOT
- DOCTOR
- DROP
- FOGGY
- ROBBER
- TODDLER

103

Answer Key

Brushing Up on Short u

Name _____

Across
3. the time just before dark
4. your shortest finger
7. soft candy
8. "bone movers"

Down
1. When something won't move, it is _____.
2. to look for something
5. something held over your head in the rain
6. a group of grapes

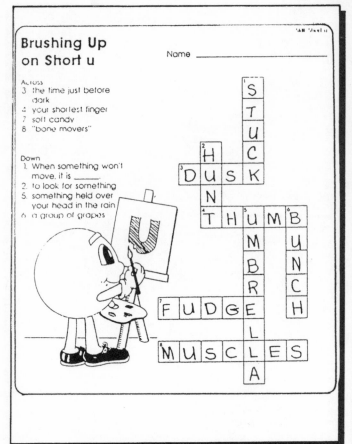

S
STUCK
²HUNT
³DUSK
⁴THUMB ⁶BUNCH
UNCH
MBRELA
⁷FUDGE
⁸MUSCLES

Grade A Work!

Name _____

Across
1. where something is located
2. Your tongue is used for this.
4. to run after something
5. traveling in a boat with sails
6. a long reptile with no legs

Down
1. a round, flat dish
3. your class in school
4. something used for coloring a picture

¹PLACE
LATE
²TASTING ³GRAD
RAD
⁴CHASE
⁵SAILING
AYO
⁶SNAKE

The Long E Beast

Name _____

Across
3. a dairy food
4. 2 + 1
6. a noise made by a pig
7. an animal that gives wool

Down
1. a good-manners word
2. a grain that flour is made from
5. to stretch to get something
6. it comes from boiling water

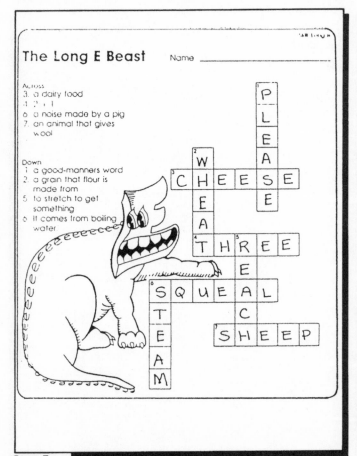

¹PLEASE
²WEAT
³CHEESE
⁴THREE
⁵SQUEAL
⁶STEAM
⁷SHEEP

Hiding Behind Long I

Name _____

Across
2. making a car go
3. a short time
4. having stripes
7. more dry

Down
1. electricity in the sky
4. a happy face
5. extinct, huge reptile
6. fastened with string

¹LIGHTNING
²DRIVING
³AWHILE
⁴STRIPED
SMILE ⁵DINOSAUR
⁶TIE
⁷DRIER

Answer Key

Bowling with Long O

Name _____

Across
1. a round model of the earth
2. They keep you warm.
4. a small rock
5. not working anymore
7. an animal with rough, brown skin

Down
1. spirits or goblins
3. more cold
5. bread eaten at breakfast

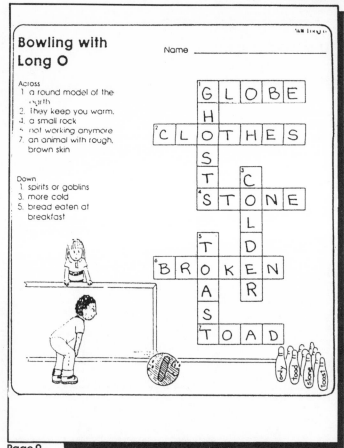

Puzzle answers:
- GLOBE
- CLOTHES
- STONE
- BROKEN
- TOAD
- GHOST (down)
- COLDER (down)
- TOAST (down)

Super U

Name _____

Across
2. a student in school
3. an honest answer
5. beautiful sound made by singing
7. to spoil something
8. a long pipe

Down
1. apples, oranges, and bananas
4. an imaginary horse-like animal with one horn
6. a set of clothes

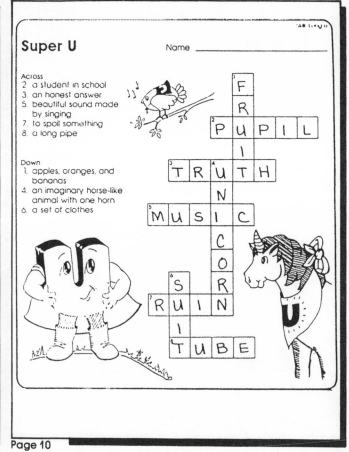

Puzzle answers:
- FRUIT
- PUPIL
- TRUTH
- MUSIC
- RUIN
- TUBE
- UNICORN (down)
- SUIT (down)

Compound Crossword

Name _____

Across
2. perhaps
4. somebody
5. a man made of snow
7. lightning bug

Down
1. to the inside of
3. a sport played with a bat, ball, and glove
5. star-shaped sea animal
6. weight used by weight-lifters

Puzzle answers:
- MAYBE
- SOMEONE
- SNOWMAN
- FIREFLY
- INTO (down)
- BASEBALL (down)
- STARFISH (down)
- BARBELL (down)

Blooming Blends

Name _____

Across
3. to shine with quick little lights
4. the funny person in the circus
5. purple or green fruit that grows in a bunch
7. to let go of

Down
1. Put this on a letter for postage.
2. blossoms
5. shining in the dark
6. how you feel when you do something special

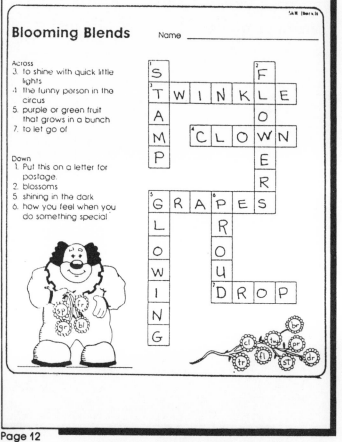

Puzzle answers:
- STAMP
- TWINKLE
- CLOWN
- GRAPES
- DROP
- FLOWER (down)
- GLOWING (down)
- PROUD (down)

Answer Key

Sharp Shooters

Name _____

Across
1. a solid dairy food
4. a hen or rooster
6. a little store
7. using something with a friend

Down
2. something worn on your feet
3. the front part of your body, above your waist
5. deciding what you want
7. having a pointed end

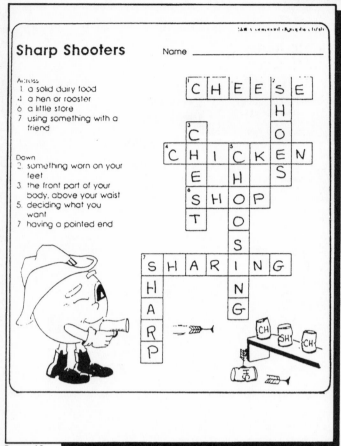

Across: 1. CHEESE, 4. CHICKEN, 6. SHOP, 7. SHARING
Down: 2. SHOES, 3. CHEST, 5. CHOOSING, 7. SHARP

Page 13

The "ing" Things

Name _____

Across
3. putting your hands together to make a sound
4. twirling around like a top
6. thinking first about how to do something
7. receiving

Down
1. coming in first place
2. tapping lightly
5. making a quick, sharp sound

Across: 3. CLAPPING, 4. SPINNING, 6. PLANNING, 7. GETTING
Down: 1. WINNING, 2. PATTING, 5. POPPING

Page 14

Missing E Mystery!

Name _____

Across
4. going from one place to another
6. the opposite of taking
7. clearing leaves away with a tool

Down
1. sitting on something while it is going
2. what you are doing when you give part of your lunch away
3. what the sun is doing
5. moving smoothly on snow or ice

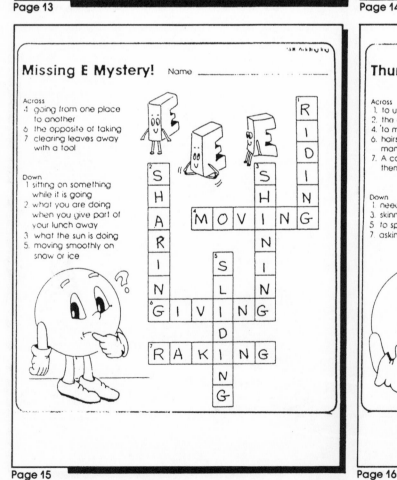

Across: 4. MOVING, 6. GIVING, 7. RAKING
Down: 1. RIDING, 2. SHARING, 3. SHINING, 5. SLIDING

Page 15

Thumbs Up!

Name _____

Across
1. to use your brain
2. the color of snow
4. to melt snow or ice
6. hairs growing on a man's face
7. A car sits on four of them.

Down
1. needing a drink
3. skinnier
5. to speak very softly
7. asking the reason

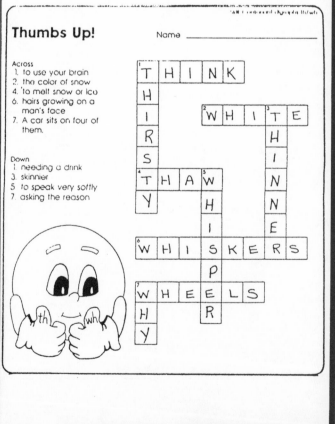

Across: 1. THINK, 2. WHITE, 4. THAW, 6. WHISKERS, 7. WHEELS
Down: 1. THIRSTY, 3. THINNER, 5. WHISPER, 7. WHY

Page 16

Answer Key

Perfect Pairs

Name _____

Across
4. hugs and _____
5. paper and _____
6. bread and _____
8. sugar and _____

Down
1. _____ and Jill
2. _____ and jelly
3. _____ and bat
7. _____ and socks

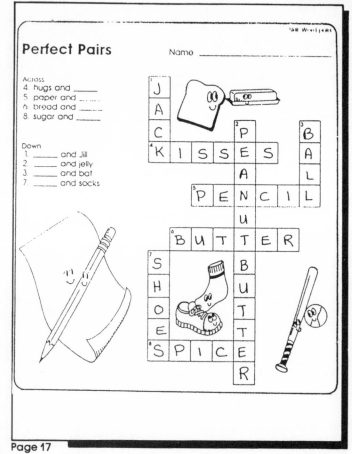

Page 17

Math Adds Up to Fun!

Name _____

Across
3. how much something is worth
4. each of two numbers you add together
6. In 27, the 2 is in the _____ place.
8. the symbol for a number

Down
1. In 201, the 2 is in the _____ place
2. to take away, as 5 - 3 = 2
5. the sign =
7. the answer you get when you add
9. to put numbers together, as 9 + 6 = 15

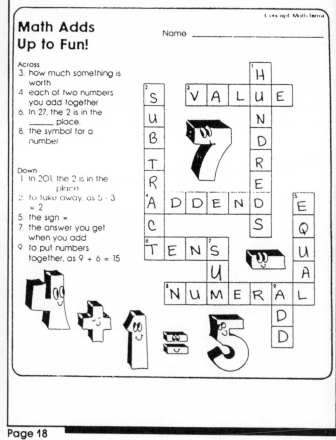

Page 18

School Tools

Name _____

Across
1. sheets of paper fastened together
2. class in school
4. used to remove pencil marks
6. colors to mix with a brush and water

Down
1. a person who teaches
2. helps stick things together
3. a colored, waxy stick used for drawing
5. a tool used for cutting
6. a sheet to write or draw on

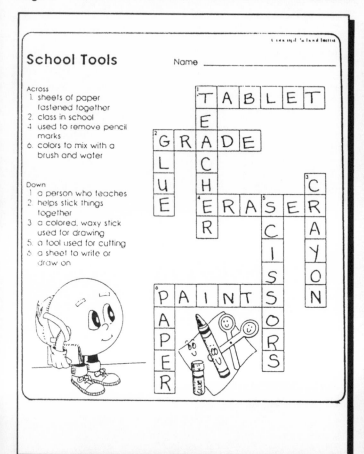

Page 19

A Is a Blast!

Name _____

Help this rocket blast-off from its launching pad by circling the short a words.

Page 20

Answer Key

In the Swim!

Name _____

Dip in and swim.
Circle the short i words in blue!

"Best in the West"

Name _____

Howdy, Partner!
Be the "best in
the west" and
pass this test. Get
your pencil ready
to circle these
short e words.

Sock Hop

Name _____

Sock it to me!
Circle the
short o words
in the puzzle.

Just Ducky!

Name _____

Jump in and
circle the short u
words.
Watch out for the
puddles!

Answer Key

Train Game

Name _____

Stop, look, and listen for the long a words in the puzzle. Circle them.

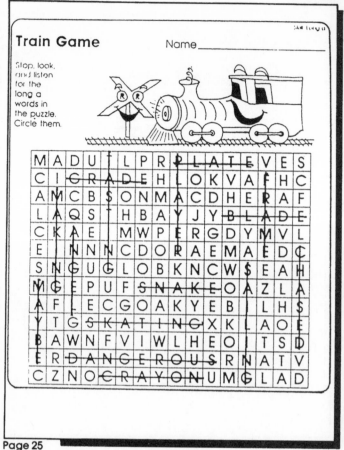

```
M A D U T L P R P L A T E V E S
C I G R A D E H L O K V A F H C
A M C B S O N M A C D H E R A F
L A Q S T H B A Y J Y B L A D E
C K A E M W P E R G D Y M V L
E I N N C D O R A E M A E D C
S N G U G L O B K N C W S E A H
M G E P U F S N A K E O A Z L A
A F L E C G O A K Y E B I L H S
Y T G S K A T I N G X K L A O E
B A W N F V I W L H E O I T S D
E R D A N G E R O U S R N A T V
C Z N O C R A Y O N U M G L A D
```

Page 25

Sweet Treats

Name _____

Treat yourself to a puzzle that you can lick! Circle the long e words in green.

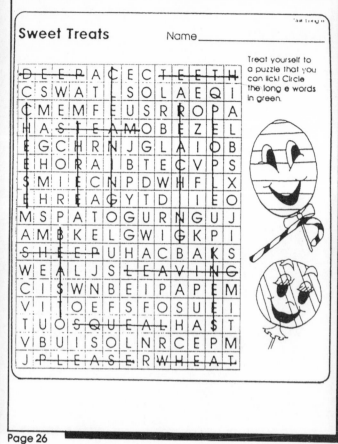

```
D E E P A C E C T E E T H
C S W A T S O L A E Q I
C M E M F E U S R R O P A
H A S T E A M O B E Z E L
E G C H R N J G L A I O B
E H O R A I B T E C V P S
S M I E C N P D W H F L X
E H R E A G Y T D I E O
M S P A T O G U R N G U J
A M B K E L G W I G K P I
S H E E P U H A C B A K S
W E A L J S L E A V I N G
C I S W N B E I P A P E M
V I T O E F S F O S U E I
T U O S Q U E A L H A S T
V B U I S O L N R C E P M
J P L E A S E R W H E A T
```

Page 26

Flying High!

Name _____

Flying high in the sky. Looking for the words with long i. Circle them

```
F S I B L K I T E S A N M I U L
L Y S G R L L V C Q J I H N E F
E T S A H Y A P S M N I B F I
G R W H I D I N G O G T S W R N
H W E H G A O Y B R H P R R D
T K G N I M Q P D E I O S I P
N O A E B T U H L G I A T O N
D M A G J I K N E H S F E U G
N M L E R O T I O U T M I G T H
G E S M I L E N S O S B A C A I
L V S O H R G E A H S T R I P E
O X S L I D E F U S F X I Z P T
D R I V I N G A R Y A Q U I E T
```

Page 27

Ghost Hosts!

Name _____

Most ghosts are noble hosts. They'll float and boast. From coast to coast, About the ghost Who finds the most. Finds what? Why, the long o words. Now you find them and circle them.

```
F E L G H O S T S Z I H O
L T N A L P E R P O F O N Y
O G T O A D L E N F A P Y
A X S I U O C H T A P I O
T Y P O B A L Z O E O N B
E G O V O N O I A H S G N
D O M G W A T Z S H I A T
E N B O L G H L T U W F L
R L W G H E V S T O N E
I Y C R N X S A L B W A N
Z O G E G R O C E R I E S
O U L H W S I W R O O P L
T N O D B R O K E N B G R
F L B A U G O L D E R K O
S N E U G M R B O N L D P
B H G J O K I N G O V A E
R I S P E L K V R A M O D
```

Page 28

Answer Key

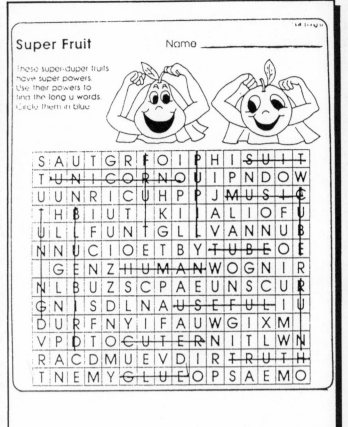

Super Fruit

Name _____

These super-duper fruits
have super powers.
Use their powers to
find the long u words.
Circle them in blue.

Compound Hound!

Name _____

Put your nose to
the ground and
"sniff" out these
compound
words.

Blending Bloomers

Name _____

Blending Bloomers will
blush and blossom as
you circle these words
with blooming blends.
Circle the blends in
blue or black.

Choose New Shoes!

Name _____

Choosing new
shoes is a chance
for a change.
Check the shop
shelves for ch/sh
words. Charge!

110

Answer Key

Double Bubbles!   Name_____

Double your fun by circling the words with double consonants. Then use a crayon to circle just the root word.

Up, Up, and Away!   Name_____

The final **e** in each of these words has blown away to make room for ing. Find the ing words in the wordsearch.

Page 33

Page 34

"Dear Deer..."   Name_____

Think About This!   Name_____

Think about which of these words begin with th or wh. Where are they? Find them in the wordsearch.

Page 35

Page 36

Answer Key

Prize-Winning Pairs   Name_____

Find those first-place pairs. Circle.

Math Matters!   Name_____

Math is "sum" fun! Find the math words in this wordsearch.

School Is Cool!   Name_____

Off to school to find these words. Up and down, they're words you've heard.

HEAP GOOD!   Name_____

Use words from the Word Bank to finish the riddle. Then use the same words to complete the puzzle.

Question

What do you call a ④ **haunted** ① **wigwam**?

Answer

A ③ **Creepy** ② **Teepee**!

Answer Key

MUMMY MADNESS

Name_____

Use words from the Word Bank to finish the riddle. Then use the same words to complete the puzzle.

Question

How can ③ y o u tell if ④ m u m m i e s have ② c o l d s?

Answer:

They ⑤ s t a r t ④ C o f f i n.

Puzzle letters:
c o l d s / c o f f i n / m u m m i e s / y o u / s t a r t

Page 41

TURKEY TALK

Name_____

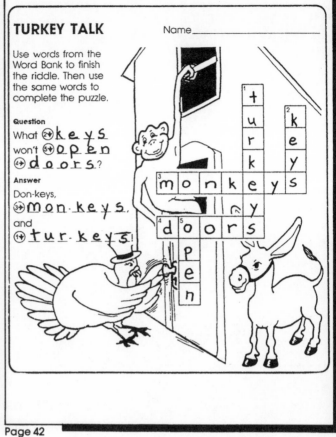

Use words from the Word Bank to finish the riddle. Then use the same words to complete the puzzle.

Question

What ② k e y s won't ⑤ o p e n ④ d o o r s?

Answer

Don-keys, ③ m o n k e y s, and ① t u r k e y s!

Puzzle: turkey / key / monkeys / doors / open

Page 42

STICKY BUSINESS

Name_____

Use words from the Word Bank to finish the riddle. Then use the same words to complete the puzzle.

Question

What do you get when you cross ⑤ p e a n u t butter with a ② t u r k e y?

Answer

A turkey that ① s t i c k s to the roof of ③ y o u r ④ m o u t h.

Puzzle: Sticks / turkey / your / mouth / peanut

Page 43

MERRY "KISS"-MOOSE!

Name_____

Use words from the Word Bank to finish the riddle. Then use the same words to complete the puzzle.

Question

Why did the ② m o o s e get ④ k i s s e d on ③ C h r i s t m a s?

Answer

He was ⑤ s t a n d i n g under the ① m o o s t l e-toe!

Puzzle: moose / most / Christmas / kissed / standing

Page 44

Crosswords and Wordsearches IF8724   113   © 1990 Instructional Fair, Inc.

Answer Key

'TWAS THE NIGHT BEFORE CHRISTMAS...

Name_____

Use words from the Word Bank to finish the riddle. Then use the same words to complete the puzzle.

Question:
What **⑤snack** do **③ducks** and **⑥cows** leave for **④Santa** Claus on Christmas **⑥Eve?**

Answer:
②Quackers and milk!

Page 45

LEAPING LEPRECHAUNS

Name_____

Use words from the Word Bank to finish the riddle. Then use the same words to complete the puzzle.

Question
What did the **④leprechaun** do **⑤when** he stubbed his **②toe?**

Answer
He called a toe- **③truck** to take him to the **④doctor.**

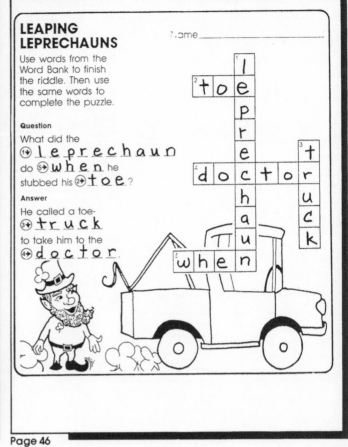

Page 46

"HARE'S" TO YOU!

Name_____

Use words from the Word Bank to finish the riddle. Then use the same words to complete the puzzle.

Question
Which Easter song is the **②favorite** of all **⑤rabbits?**

Answer
④Hare comes **⑤Peter** Cottontail, **①hopping** down the bunny trail.

Page 47

BUNNY TALES

Name_____

Use words from the Word Bank to finish the riddle. Then use the same words to complete the puzzle.

Question
How do **④rabbits** like to **②eat** their **⑤eggs?**

Answer
④Bunny **③side** up!

Page 48

Answer Key

SCHOOL'S OUT!

Name_____

Use words from the Word Bank to finish the riddle. Then use the same words to complete the puzzle.

Question

Why is
① s c h o o l
out at three
② o'c l o c k ?

Answer

Because the bell strikes one,
③ s t r i k e s
two, strikes three — and
④ y o u are
③ o u t !

Crossword answers:
- 1 across: S C H O O L
- 2 down: C L O C K
- 3 down: O U T
- 4 across: Y O U
- 5 across: S T R I K E S

Page 49

Noun Search

Name_____

Find the noun in each sentence.

Across
3. The chocolate cookies are crumbly.
5. The princess went shopping.

Down
1. Tip the box over.
2. We are sitting on the bicycle.
4. They were going to paint the building.
5. Watch the pony trot.
6. Getting the extra cupcake in was not easy.
7. I almost lost my skates.

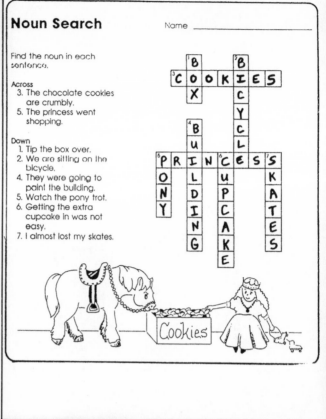

Crossword answers:
- 1 down: BOX
- 2 down: BICYCLE
- 3 across: COOKIES
- 4 down: BUILDING
- 5 across: PRINCESS
- 6 down: PONY / CUPCAKE
- 7 down: SKATES

Cookies

Page 50

Verb Search

Name_____

Find the verb in each sentence.

Across
2. The coyote howled at the moon.
4. My sister laughs at my jokes.
5. My friend visits me on the weekend.
7. A mule kicks with the hind legs.

Down
1. My mom works in a grocery store.
3. Mr. Jones drives our school bus.
4. The horses live in the stable.
6. He always trips over his shoe laces.

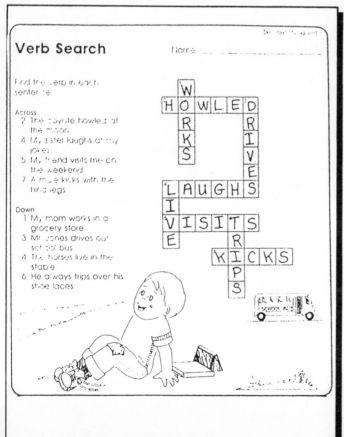

Crossword answers:
- 1 down: WORKS
- 2 across: HOWLED
- 3 down: DRIVE
- 4 across: LAUGHS / 4 down: LIVE
- 5 across: VISITS
- 6 down: TRIPS
- 7 across: KICKS

SCHOOL BUS

Page 51

Proper Shoppers

Name_____

Change these proper nouns to common nouns

Across
2. Ford, Chevrolet, Toyota
5. Christmas or Halloween
7. California
8. Park Place, Lane Avenue, Willow Blvd

Down
1. Abe Lincoln, George Washington, Ronald Reagan
3. Wednesday or Saturday
4. Africa, Asia, North America
6. Atlantic, Pacific, Arctic, Indian

Crossword answers:
- 1 down: PRESIDENTS
- 2 across: CARS
- 3 down: DAY
- 4 down: CONTINENTS
- 5 across: HOLIDAY
- 6 down: OCEANS
- 7 across: STATE
- 8 across: STREETS

HOLIDAY PRESENTS CONTINENTS

Page 52

Punctuation Puffins

Skill: Function of punctuation marks

Name _____

Across
2. A question mark (?) is used with sentences that _____
4. Commas (,) are _____
7. An apostrophe (') in a contraction shows that a letter has been left _____
8. Quotation marks (" ") are placed around what someone _____

Down
1. Hyphens (-) are similar to _____
3. A period (.) comes at the end of a _____
5. Exclamation points (!) show _____
6. A colon (:) is used before a _____ of things.

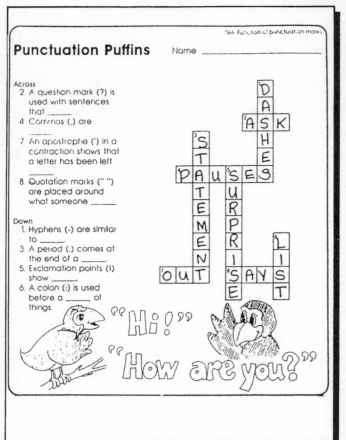

Crossword answers:
- DASHES
- ASK
- STATEMENT
- PAUSES
- SURPRISE
- OUT
- SAYS
- LIST

"Hi!" "How are you?"

A Zoo for Two

Skill: Identifying 2-syllable words

Name _____

Find the 2-syllable words.

Across
2. horse–catfish–antelope
3. rabbit–ape–hare
4. elephant–otter–pelican
7. hippopotamus–quail–walrus

Down
1. kitten–dog–lamb
3. kangaroo–ant–raccoon
5. hummingbird–eagle–frog
6. rhinoceros–sheep–cougar

Crossword answers:
- KITTEN
- CATFISH
- RABBIT
- RACCOON
- OTTER
- EAGLE
- COUGAR
- WALRUS

Contraction Actions

Skill: Contractions

Name _____

Write the words which form the contractions

Across
2. She's not home right now.
3. He'd like to go to the game.
5. They're all gone!
7. He's my best friend.

Down
1. I'll go get the pizza.
4. My friend doesn't live next door any more.
5. They've moved three times.
6. You've never been to the zoo.

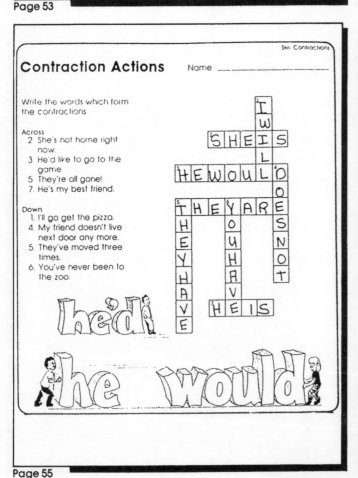

Crossword answers:
- I WILL
- SHE IS
- HE WOULD
- THEY ARE
- THEY HAVE
- YOU HAVE
- DOES NOT
- HE IS

he'd — he would

Ordinals, Ordinals

Skill: Ordinal numbers

Name _____

Write the ordinals.

Across
2. before second
3. three before thirteenth
7. two after ninth
8. between second and fourth

Down
1. eight before fourteenth
4. four after sixteenth
5. nine before thirteenth
6. between first and third

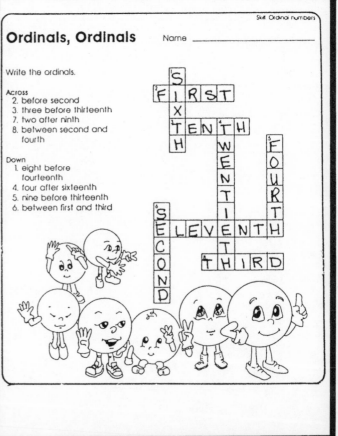

Crossword answers:
- FIRST
- SIXTH
- TENTH
- TWENTIETH
- FOURTH
- SECOND
- ELEVENTH
- THIRD

Answer Key

Shapes

Name _____

What is the shape?

across:

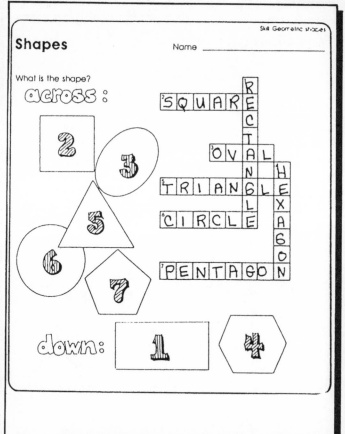

¹SQUARE

²RECTANGLE

³OVAL

⁵TRIANGLE / HEXAGON

⁶CIRCLE

⁷PENTAGON

down:

Page 57

For Good Measure

Name _____

What is the measurement term?

Across
2. degrees in the metric system
4. There are 4 in one quart
5. There are 12 in one foot
8. 3 feet make 1 of these

Down
1. metric liquid measurement
3. Twelve inches make one.
4. 100 of them make a meter
5. There are 2 in one quart

²CELSIUS / ¹LITERS

⁶FOOT / ³CENTIMETERS / ⁵PINT

⁶OUNCES

⁷INCHES

YARD

Page 58

Just In Time

Name _____

Across
2. February is the only _____ with 28 days
5. 10 years
7. 60 seconds make 1

Down
1. a celebration of 100 years
3. 365 days equal 1 _____
4. 100 years
6. There are 52 in a year.

²CENTENNIAL

³MONTH

⁵DECADE / ⁴CENTURY

³YEAR / ⁶WEEKS

⁷MINUTE

Page 59

Math Fun

Name _____

Across
2. In 6 + 7 = 13, the 6 and 7 are the _____
4. 8 + 7 = 15 is an _____
6. a part of a whole

Down
1. to put numbers together as 7 + 9 = 16
3. guessing how many there are
5. In 16 ÷ 8 = 2, 2 is called the _____
6. In 5 x 6 = 30, the 5 or 6 is called a _____
7. the outside surface of something

¹ADD / ²ADDENDS

⁴EQUATION

⁶FRACTION / ⁵QUOTIENT

FACTOR / AREA

Page 60

Answer Key

Did You Brush?

Name _____

Across
3. the back, grinding teeth
5. added to water and toothpaste to help prevent decay
7. the inner part of the tooth containing the nerves
8. His tooth hurt or _____

Down
1. the place where teeth are anchored by the roots
2. invisible, sticky material on your teeth which causes decay
4. double-pointed tooth that tears food
5. a string used to clean between the teeth
6. hard, white outer surface of teeth

Trees and Leaves

Name _____

How well do you know your trees?

Across
1. the home of acorns
2. has nuts that are delicious when roasted
5. huge trees found in California

Down
1. The leaf of this tree is Canada's national symbol
3. an evergreen tree
4. has red wood that is used to make chests for storing linens
5. a hardwood shade tree
6. has long, graceful branches that often touch the ground

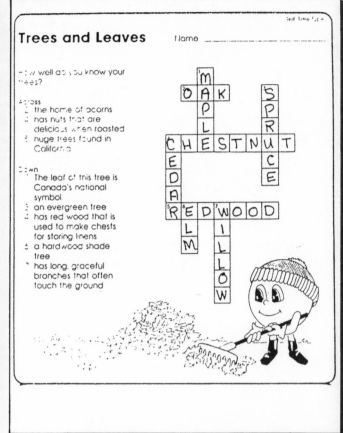

Leaping Lizards!

Name _____

Across
2. In Tyrannosaurus Rex, the Rex means _____
4. The "tri" in Triceratops means it has _____ horns
5. Stegosaurus had sharp _____ on its tail
6. Some dinosaurs had bills like a _____

Down
1. The "saur" in dinosaur means _____
3. Stegosaurus had hard, bony _____ on its back
4. From Greek, the "dino" in dinosaur means _____
5. There are no more dinosaurs, they are _____

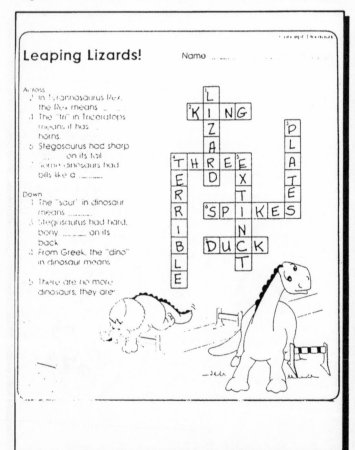

The Daily News

Name _____

Across
1. information about what has just happened
3. the person who edits the newspaper
5. the condition of the air from day to day
6. lists and page numbers of parts of the paper
7. advertisements

Down
2. baseball, football, soccer
4. a special interest story found in the newspaper
6. newspaper cartoons

Crosswords and Wordsearches IF8724   118   © 1990 Instructional Fair, Inc.

Answer Key

Orbiting in Space

Name

Across
2. Earth's sister planet, surrounded by clouds
3. the path a planet travels around the sun
4. the planet closest to the sun
6. the "Red Planet"
7. the eighth planet from the sun

Down
1. the largest planet in the solar system
5. the seventh planet in the solar system

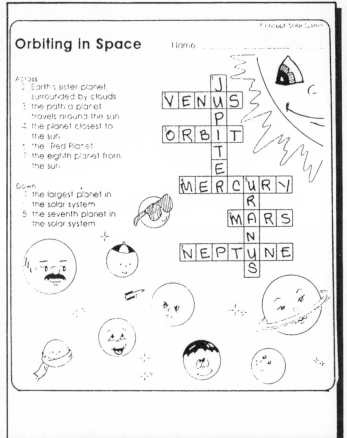

Crossword answers:
VENUS
ORBIT
JUPITER
MERCURY
URANUS
MARS
NEPTUNE

The Noun Clown

Name

No clowning! You'll do well circling the 15 nouns in this wordsearch.

The Verb Van

Name

Get your wheels rolling! Verbs are action words. Circle the 15 verbs in the wordsearch.

VERB VAN

Plural Panda-Monium

Name

Circle the plural forms of these nouns.

119

Answer Key

Here's the Pitch!　Name_____

How many proper nouns can you catch? Each common noun in the word bank has a matching proper noun in the puzzle. Circle them with your favorite color.

TUESDAY　city　day　NEW YORK　Ocean　PACIFIC

C H E V Y L D K O R T C H D F M
I S G N O P A C I F I C L A U A
B C M B N A Y Z D O I S U L J
Y E O W L V I O G D T M P L Q N
A N N O H C D G A S I A R A E S
N E D L C X A A V O S Y R S O I
K I A V R E A G A N B F M C P R
E B Y N O H F N R I Y C L O T E
Y B E A W B O H I O Z A W D E
S M C I N D Y I R S V Y N B L T
N I M K R I A J A X I C M O G A
S I H A L L O W E E N M R Y S H
J E M S A L T L A K E A K S R D

Guide Word Giraffe　Name_____

Take a LONG look... Circle only the words that would come between the guide words gape - grape in the dictionary.

N T G A S O L G I B R T G
A X L S G U E S S G E T A
Y G A T E G F E R U W B
G A M N B O N P E C G W
H I G A R D E N F T K J
O G I S G R O C Y T G A O
K I G B O I L L S E R N F
A R Y I T C O I D R I T
W A L Y B E C G A L T M I
N F E A G I G G L E S H G
E R R G T O H H Y D U V N
M E D A N L S O V G L U E
G I R V E H O S T R N U B
A W L E F D I T N E B W G
I G L A R E A G R A P H O
N E O W G Y I M A S O T T
P L I W L G R A I N O L K

Punctuation Notation!　Name_____

Skill: Function of punctuation marks

"Tune in" on punctuation marks. Circle the names of 10 punctuation marks in this wordsearch. When do you use each mark?

Q A H Y P H E N N Q Z C T U V H
U U Z E C B S I G U M A W K F T
E X C L A M A T I O N P O I N T
S Q S I P O R E J T D X E D U F
T U P D O B F P L A Y C O M M A
I T Q Y S X V A W T D E J O B I
O R E O T E S E M I C O L O N F
N R A M R V O S M O I P A G I C
M E P W O P M C O N L E Z G E K
A C A N P K O I R M Y R O J G I
R S L O H W A T K A R I H U W
K L Q U E M O N E R H O V M U L
R C O L O N L B S K N D A S H A

Ssssyllable Sssssnakes!　Name_____

"Ssss"earch for 15 snaky words that have two syllables.

F E S J U N G L E O V G N
C U A D N P O O D E M O
O S T Q U A B L M E R K V
B R O E C R A T T L E K L
R I B B O N M M A M R P H
A C I F D A E R B T R Z A
E O V M A S P O T T D R
H A R M F U L C N O P E M
F H I S S I N G J K S L
V I G K N A Y F G L X E
P U Q L E Y M O A G L N S
H P E C M A L E G L D S S
B Y U L O D T O A S M C H
P T A E M I C K R E Y P U
E H O O N O S E T G U E P
M O Y E R E K T E H Y A G
A N S L I T H E R N H L A

Answer Key

Catching Contractions!

Name_____

Find the contractions for the words in the word bank. You will have to add the missing apostrophes. Try to get a perfect score.

```
Y A D O L N I T E H A L V O B C
O W O N T E T A I E C F G U B R
U R N I E L S W O D O E S N T O
S U T C A L T U X I F A C G N D
T E W L N D O K J O M Y S C B I
T H E Y V E G W A C M O G T M D
O N T A L N T E W L C U I E R N
R I C B E A Y N D O N R K E W I
N H R E I S N T N C K E O G R E
W L G E L I Y B E K R K I V E B
H K A D B O A Z N E G I L M S A
O L T H E Y R E F I E D L P O F
S L A U P F N O J Y O U V E R T
```

Ordinal Orchestra!

Name_____

Get with the beat! Ordinal numbers show order. Circle an ordinal number for each number in the word bank.

```
D S I O S T W A K Y R O U
U N S I X T E E N T H D
W X H E T L H E N W I E
N T D V G O C G T E A O
E H C E O N R C H A N N U
N B R N I D I U N T E R
I A R T H W E A H M I M T
N U T H S R E B W I K E S H
T A S C H O N T O S T E K
H R J K Y A T E N T H M
T I A B S C H O S U G O M
I F K L E L E V E N T H J
W T S A C H O I R S E L T
S H R E O D S V K S I C N
O M A C N T W E L F T H L
T H I R D E P A K C L T Y
P G E N R C A H F I R S T
```

first *second* *third*

Ship Shape!

Name_____

Ahoy, matey! Circle the names of the geometric shapes in the wordsearch. Can you draw the shapes?

```
P O C U B E W S N H B A L R G O
A O Y P G P H T Y E S P R I S M
R I L C R S E R T K R E M S P O
A M P E A H I S A I N E F H G
L Y N U C R C A E G F T A L E R
L F D A T I R N A O F A S Y R O
E L E O A K A G N N E G B I E S
L C R B N A M L O I C O N E W O
O C T A G O N E S U L N M C D V
G T I G L N G N C I R C L E L A
R S U A E M I T O S N S M U B L
A W V C E S K E P Y R A M I D M
M C S Q U A R E H M I S U T B Y
```

How do you measure up?

Name_____

The abbreviations in the word bank are for measurement words. Find those words in the wordsearch and circle in brown.

```
W A F I N C C E L S I U S
O I N C H H O Z I D L A R
R S V M G R A M T O D M C
O T I E H L A R E D I B E
U C E T V Q W I R N W S N
N F A E X U D U C G H Y T
D E C R H A P U C A P E I
H A J Y O R H Y N L G O M
I G P N O T O C W L O L E
K I L O G R A M E O T X T
Y F A E S P B V S N A B E
P O L O U N C E K B Q U R
E O P V I F Y U L M S A F
C T I D W K E B E Y A R D
V H O S P I N T C A Y F S
O W F T A E X P I L T V J
A F A H R E N H E I T B K
```

Answer Key

Time's Up!

Name_____

Measuring time can make you "tick." Search for these "timely" answers in the puzzle.

E	C	T	O	D	W	A	B	Y	S	B	R	W	E	E	K
H	T	D	A	Y	B	M	O	E	A	I	L	W	P	N	A
A	E	F	Y	D	U	I	N	A	K	C	Y	G	J	I	H
L	C	I	L	R	E	N	S	F	L	E	A	L	N	I	A
F	L	M	G	O	F	U	T	I	B	N	P	O	Y	X	L
H	O	U	R	F	U	C	L	D	T	S	Z	R	O	F	F
O	D	P	I	L	C	F	W	T	C	E	O	P	U	J	M
U	L	S	W	K	I	C	L	C	E	N	T	U	R	Y	L
R	D	E	C	A	D	E	A	D	N	N	G	I	C	L	N
M	A	V	G	B	I	F	G	C	E	I	K	N	A	H	U
S	I	M	H	C	O	E	B	Y	E	A	R	W	E	P	E
V	M	O	N	T	H	K	O	R	G	L	N	A	P	G	E
O	S	M	A	C	Y	I	L	G	E	H	S	E	O	R	A

Page 77

"Term"-inal Math!

Name_____

Find these math terms in the puzzle. Be ready to tell what each term means.

A	R	E	A	O	U	N	R	P	D	G	N	I
G	R	E	G	R	O	U	P	E	Q	S	U	M
F	U	M	P	V	I	S	N	R	O	A	P	E
R	A	D	D	E	N	D	Z	I	C	Q	N	E
A	D	T	O	A	N	G	M	K	U	J	S	T
C	U	F	A	C	T	O	R	B	U	O	T	T
I	F	P	O	L	S	W	T	B	T	V	I	I
I	G	E	L	N	H	Y	A	E	R	I	Q	M
O	C	R	M	G	I	M	G	R	U	E	D	A
N	A	E	T	R	C	M	B	V	I	N	F	T
A	S	N	B	U	K	E	F	I	F	T	O	O
M	I	C	S	E	G	I	O	D	E	N	I	N
G	U	E	R	N	I	R	C	B	Y	O	Z	G
P	N	E	O	T	L	Y	M	A	Z	O	P	R
U	M	Y	E	T	M	S	E	G	M	E	N	T
V	O	L	U	M	E	H	T	S	E	C	F	L
A	E	R	A	G	T	P	R	O	D	U	C	T

$6 \div 2 =$

$\begin{array}{r} 4 \\ \times 3 \end{array}$

$\begin{array}{r} 3 \\ -2 \end{array}$

$\begin{array}{r} 4 \\ +4 \end{array}$

Page 78

The "Brush-Off"!

Name_____

"Brush up" on these dental health words. Mr. Tooth is "rooting" for you to find all 15 words.

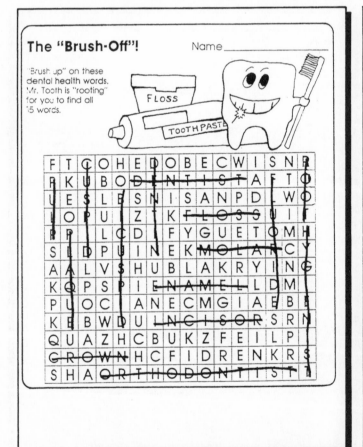

FLOSS
TOOTHPASTE

F	T	C	O	H	E	D	O	B	E	C	W	I	S	N	R
R	K	U	B	O	D	N	T	I	S	T	A	F	T	O	
U	E	S	L	E	S	N	I	S	A	N	P	D	L	W	O
I	O	P	U	Z	T	K	F	L	O	S	S	U	I	T	
R	P	L	C	D	F	Y	G	U	E	T	O	M	H		
S	L	D	P	U	I	N	E	K	M	O	L	A	R	C	Y
A	A	L	V	S	H	U	B	L	A	K	R	Y	I	N	G
K	O	P	S	P	I	E	N	A	M	E	L	L	D	M	
P	U	O	C	A	N	E	C	M	G	I	A	E	B		
K	E	B	W	D	U	L	N	C	I	S	O	R	S	R	N
Q	U	A	Z	H	C	B	U	K	Z	F	E	I	L	P	
G	R	O	W	N	H	C	F	I	D	R	E	N	K	R	S
S	H	A	O	R	T	H	O	D	O	N	T	I	S	T	

Page 79

Trees...A Breeze!

Name_____

You are TREE...mendous! Find the names of 15 different kinds of trees. Can you identify their leaves?

M	A	S	C	F	I	R	H	I	V	Y	E	O
M	D	Y	A	L	B	E	L	F	E	B	W	J
Q	U	C	E	D	A	R	Y	A	L	F	I	U
B	E	A	H	M	U	B	R	N	M	V	C	N
H	E	M	L	O	C	K	H	I	C	E	L	I
U	R	O	A	C	O	K	I	P	S	A	E	P
M	O	R	E	D	W	O	O	D	E	P	U	E
Y	L	E	I	C	M	A	I	S	L	R	L	R
P	O	R	L	O	C	U	S	T	U	O	D	A
W	I	L	L	O	W	I	R	M	X	F	D	O
S	P	I	C	R	U	E	R	T	P	L	O	D
O	D	L	A	R	P	I	N	E	G	A	U	F
A	W	A	M	R	O	T	C	U	Y	R	G	I
K	O	U	C	P	E	S	P	R	U	C	E	D
X	E	R	B	F	T	A	C	E	S	B	V	Q
C	H	E	S	T	N	U	T	H	I	A	C	S
N	O	I	M	A	I	T	O	M	A	P	L	E

Page 80

122

Answer Key

The Space Place!

Name_____

"Blast-off" into this space wordsearch. "Launch" your mind to find 15 space words. Can you define them?

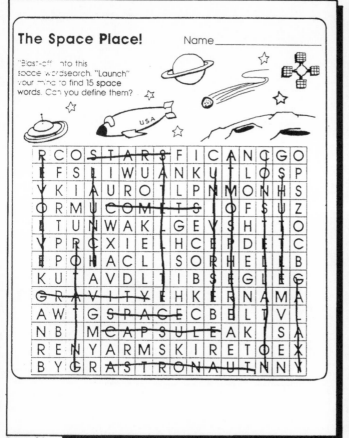

```
R C O S T A R S F I C A N G O
E F S L I W U A N K U T L O S P
Y K I A U R O T L P N M O N H S
O R M U C O M E T S O F S U Z
E T U N W A K L G E V S H T O
V P R O X I E L H C E P D E T C
E P O H A C L S O R H E L L B
K U T A V D L T I B S E G L E G
G R A V I T Y E H K E R N A M A
A W T G S P A C E C B E L T V L
N B M C A P S U L E A K S A
R E N Y A R M S K I R E T O E X
B Y G R A S T R O N A U T N N Y
```

Dynamite Dinosaurs!

Name_____

These beasts of "extinct"-tion are lost. Can you find all 10 of them?

```
L W D A O T R S E C A Y L
T R I C E R A T O P S G B
Y O P F S A R E G T C U R
P P L I A C F G O E S D O
A V O G E H V O E R D W N
N E D U P C B S I O C M T
N U O A S D K A R D F I O
O I C N L C S U W A D N S
S G L O P N A R J C E P A
A Y S D M E C U W T H E U
U A L O R J V S K Y V O R
R B E N U S R C I L U N U
S V P S J M I A N L O S
S O A L L O S A U R U S Y
C G T E L A L C B W U V D
B R A C H I O S A U R U S
A F I K N A Y U G H O Q A
```

Extra! Extra! Read All About It!

Name_____

These newspaper words are "hot off the press." Circle them and then find them in your newspaper.

```
B I F L C O M I C S B W C
S A N W L A D V I C E S S
P M F E A T U R E S H A P
O H B A S R E L X P S T O
R N U B S O S B I R T H S
T D S V E I F A P R E O
S T U F B G C D A N R I
C V N M E A L E R Y P N
E G E H E L P W A N T E D
L U S Q D O U L T I G Y E
P S K A H J E H S C T X
A D R E D H W O S R E V I
W E L I S O X B O S L A N
E N T E R T A I N M E N T
P I A T F C Y O W N D O B
J A H E D I T O R I A L N
W E D D I N G S G E N S O
```

All Systems Go!

Name_____

Our solar system has nine planets. Circle their names in blue. Circle the other "astro" words in yellow.

```
V I T A E A R T H C U L P H E Z
E C M I C R A S I L S A N V J K
U R A N U S O H M Q U V E N U S
M A O D C U Y H O R L D P C I A
E T M S L V I B O L U E I G B T
M E R C U R Y S N J N M U N T U
P R E Y A R Y T S O A M N D A R
T S M E J U P I T E R Y B L U N
F U R A E Y L G I O V Y M F S A
C O R B I T U B I K P L A N E T
M V A F C R T O L K N C I D W N
B P E Y S S O L A R M K A P O S
M A R S L N E V A C R E J H O M
```

Answer Key

It's Your Serve!

Name _____

Circle the sport in which each piece of equipment is used.

O	B	A	S	K	E	T	B	A	L	L	S	M	P	S	A
J	R	M	K	I	H	O	P	S	C	O	T	C	H	A	R
B	O	S		W	O	C	H	L	I	T	E	N	N	I	S
A	C	P	I	N	G	P	O	N	G	K	R	S	V	E	N
S	B	R	N	T	S	K	A	T	I	N	G	A	L	B	E
E	I	F	G	C	W	L	E	A	V	K	O	N	G	O	X
B	A	C	V	F	O	O	T	B	A	L	L	W	O	X	A
A	S	R	I	N	G	T	O	S	S	R	A	D	L	E	E
L	Y	N	U	K	L	H	O	C	K	E	Y	F	A	N	O
L	T	I	K	N	G	A	O	L	P	U	C	T	O	G	I
B	H	O	R	S	E	B	A	C	K	R	I	D	I	N	G
G	Y	M	N	A	S	T	I	C	S	E	B	N	D	O	W
K	D	S	W	I	M	M	I	N	G	C	E	L	A	O	S

Page 85

Dictionary Diploma!

Name _____

Across
1. Part of a word
3. A mini-dictionary in the back of a school text
7. The syllable that is stressed in a word
8. All dictionaries have pronounciation

Down
1. To pronounce a word
2. The word you are looking up
3. Words at the top of a dictionary page that help you find the entry word quickly
4. A noun, verb, or adverb is called a part of
5. To tell the meaning of a word
6. To give more force to a syllable

Crossword answers: SYLLABLE, ENTRY, SAY, GLOSSARY, GUIDEWORDS, SPEECH, ACCENT, DEFINE, STRESS, KEYS

Page 86

What's In a Name?

Name _____

Across
1. March is named for this Roman god of war.
3. January is named for this god of gates and doors.
5. October's origin – the Roman number 8
7. Wednesday is named for this Roman god.

Down
1. Monday's origin – the _ _ _ _'s day.
2. Sunday is named for the center of our solar system.
4. Saturday is named for this Roman god of agriculture.
6. Thursday is named for this god of thunder and lightning.

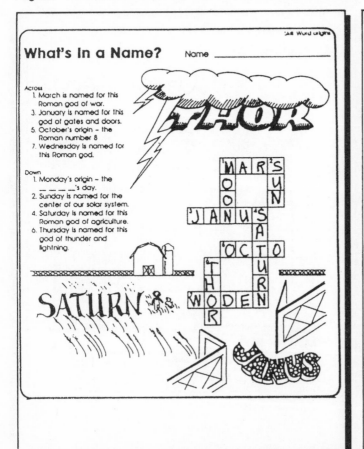

Crossword answers: MARS, SUN, MOON, JANUS, SATURN, OCTO, THOR, WODEN

Page 87

Health Helpers!

Name _____

Across
2. You need _____ to work and play.
4. Nutrient necessary for growth and good health
6. Nutrient which stores energy
7. Plants that are used as a source of food
9. Wheat, corn, rice, and oats are examples of these.
10. Foods made from milk – they are a source of calcium.
11. Your body at rest

Down
1. Steak, liver, lamb – these are good sources of iron.
3. About 60% of your body is
5. A nutrient needed for many jobs, including building strong bones and teeth
8. To make your body work

Crossword answers: ENERGY, MEAT, WATER, VITAMINS, FATS, MINERALS, VEGETABLES, EXERCISE, GRAINS, DAIRY, SLEEP

Page 88

Answer Key

Don't Pollute!

Name _____

Across
1. The wearing away of the earth by wind, water, and ice
6. This type of accident endangers ocean life.
8. The science of the relationship between living things and their environment
10. The natural, living part of our world

Down
2. Energy which is sent out from atoms and molecules as they undergo change
3. Smoke and fog
4. This makes our environment dirty and unhealthy.
5. To use something over and over again.
7. Chemicals used to control insects – they can harm plant and animal life.
9. Trash thrown about and not disposed of

Crossword answers: EROSION, RADIATION, OILSPILL, POLLUTION, PESTICIDES, RECYCLE, ECOLOGY, ENVIRONMENT, LITTER, SMOG

Page 89

Land and Water

Name _____

Across
4. One of the seven large bodies of land on the earth
8. The deep, narrow part of a waterway
9. An inland body of water
10. A great body of salt water

Down
1. High, rocky land – it usually has steep sides and a pointed or rounded top.
2. A land area with very little water or plant-life
3. A body of land almost surrounded by water
5. A large stream of water which empties into an ocean or lake
6. A level area of land found in the mountains
7. A body of land which is totally surrounded by water

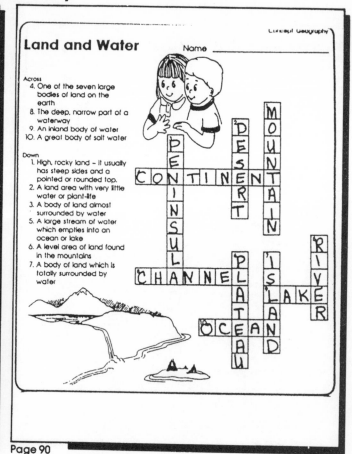

Crossword answers: MOUNTAIN, DESERT, CONTINENT, PENINSULA, CHANNEL, PLATEAU, ISLAND, RIVER, LAKE, OCEAN

Page 90

Ocean Going

Name _____

Across
2. A large area of water which extends from the ocean into the coastline
5. Its clusters of tentacles resemble flowers.
6. A large ocean which meets the western coast of the United States
9. An animal with five or more arms resembling a star
10. Ocean plant-life

Down
1. The flow of water in the ocean
3. The ocean located between North America and Europe.
4. A person who studies ocean life
7. A six-foot unit used for measuring water depth
8. A small fish that resembles a horse

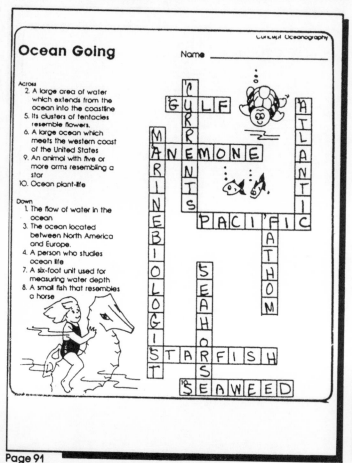

Crossword answers: GULF, CURRENT, MARINEBIOLOGIST, ANEMONE, ATLANTIC, PACIFIC, FATHOM, SEAHORSE, STARFISH, SEAWEED

Page 91

Star-Struck

Name _____

Across
1. Any object that orbits another object
4. Everything that exists
6. The path of a planet around the sun
9. The sun and all the heavenly bodies that revolve around it

Down
2. An instrument used for observing objects that are far away
3. A group of stars named after an object they resemble
5. The study of stars and planets
7. A reuseable space craft
8. A grouping of millions of stars

Crossword answers: SATELLITE, UNIVERSE, ORBIT, CONSTELLATION, TELESCOPE, ASTRONOMY, SHUTTLE, GALAXY, SOLARSYSTEM

Page 92

Answer Key

Hot Off the Press!

Name _____

Across
1. A person who reports the news
5. A major story in the newspaper
8. To prepare and sell a newspaper
9. A listing of the contents of a newspaper
10. Cartoons found in the newspaper

Down
2. An article which expresses the opinion of a newspaper's editor
3. This section tells us if we will need an umbrella
4. The top, front page title of a newspaper story
6. An agreement to receive and pay for the newspaper on a regular basis
7. The section which tells who won last night's basketball game

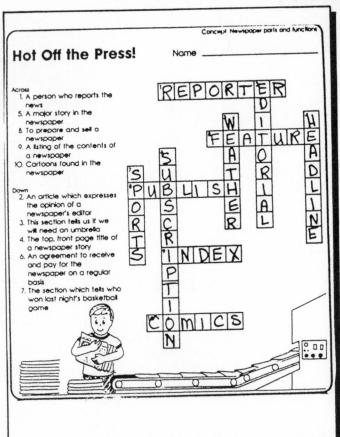

Page 93

Forests

Name _____

Across
3. Making the best use of and protecting the forests, land, and other natural resources
5. A mixture of ground up wood used for making paper
6. Layers of wood glued and pressed together
8. A place where trees are grown for harvesting
9. A substance put into the soil to give extra food to plants

Down
1. A person who is employed to guard the forest
2. A pond of water near a sawmill that is used for storing logs
4. A place where logs are sawed into boards
7. A lumberjack
8. A region near the Equator with rain forests

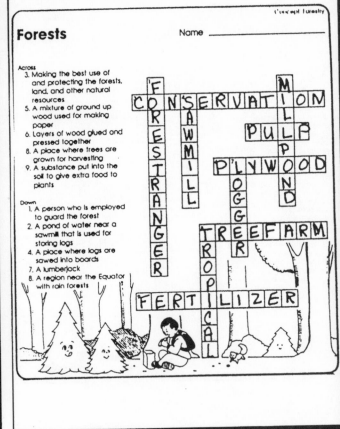

Page 94

Scary, Scary, Dictionary

Name _____

Using the dictionary does not have to be scary! Find these words in the puzzle and then tell what their job is.

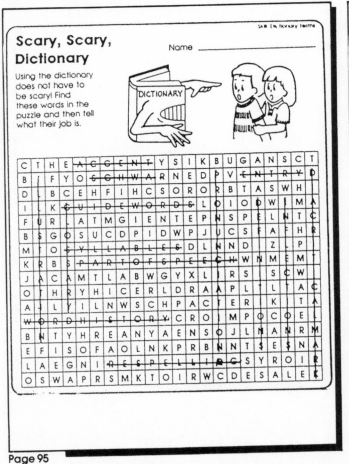

Page 95

Call It a Day!

Name _____

The names of the days and the months come from the origins listed in the Clue Bank. Match each word origin with the right name. Then find the names in the puzzle.

THANKSGIVING DAY PARADE! THOR'S DAY, NOVEM. 28

Page 96

Answer Key

Healthy and Happy! Name _____

To stay healthy, you need food, exercise, and rest. Find 17 words that are necessary for good health.

G	I	E	A	E	N	O	F	R	U	I	T	E	Y	M	T
R	P	R	O	T	E	I	N	S	V	H	E	V	A	U	Z
E	S	T	O	B	F	S	O	S	L	E	E	P	X	L	Y
R	R	R	H	I	O	R	L	E	B	A	D	C	B	K	N
R	M	D	H	O	E	E	W	M	T	O	R	B	W	P	O
O	E	E	N	V	I	T	A	M	I	N	S	F	D	R	A
F	R	O	L	R	B	E	T	E	I	V	A	E	V	O	U
S	G	A	I	C	E	R	E	A	L	N	Y	G	N	D	D
U	Y	E	A	U	G	U	R	S	T	Y	E	A	U	U	M
T	E	R	K	E	H	T	E	T	W	E	G	H	I	C	E
S	A	S	R	T	O	N	S	G	A	T	E	U	M	T	T
C	Y	T	L	W	E	I	S	H	U	R	T	I	I	S	I
M	S	O	T	A	R	C	H	I	L	A	T	N	T	R	
K	R	S	E	I	L	H	I	E	T	Y	B	J	E	O	K
E	P	M	E	A	T	O	R	I	A	I	L	I	P	S	U
I	Y	E	A	M	E	N	D	T	O	U	E	K	A	R	N
O	R	W	T	T	H	E	O	N	E	W	S	C	L	T	O
N	A	F	E	X	E	R	C	I	S	E	H	A	S	B	A
G	L	E	A	N	L	I	N	E	S	S	U	I	O	Q	O
U	O	H	N	H	G	O	Y	A	G	R	I	N	E	P	R
C	T	E	Y	C	U	Y	G	R	A	I	N	L	A	F	L

Pollution Is a Dirty Word! Name _____

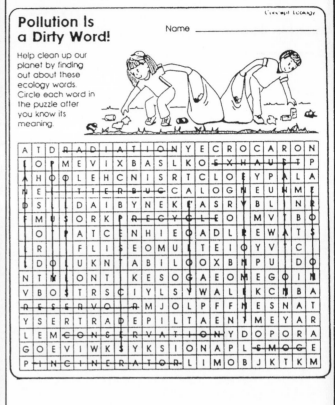

Help clean up our planet by finding out about these ecology words. Circle each word in the puzzle after you know its meaning.

A	T	D	R	A	D	I	A	T	I	O	N	Y	E	C	R	O	C	A	R	O	N
I	O	P	M	E	V	I	X	B	A	S	L	K	O	E	X	H	A	U	S	T	P
A	H	O	O	L	E	H	C	N	I	S	R	T	C	L	O	E	Y	P	A	L	A
E	E	L	L	T	T	E	R	B	U	G	C	A	L	O	G	N	E	U	N	M	E
D	S	L	L	D	A	I	B	Y	N	E	K	I	A	S	R	Y	B	L	I	N	R
F	M	U	S	O	R	K	P	R	E	C	Y	C	L	E	O	I	M	V	T	B	O
O	O	P	A	T	C	E	N	H	I	E	O	A	D	L	R	E	W	A	T	S	
R	I	F	L	I	S	E	O	M	U	L	T	E	I	O	Y	V	T	C			
D	D	O	U	K	N	T	A	B	I	L	O	O	X	B	N	P	U	D	O		
N	T	M	O	N	T	K	E	S	O	G	A	E	O	M	E	G	O	I	N		
V	B	O	S	T	R	S	C	I	Y	L	S	W	A	L	K	C	N	B	A		
R	E	S	E	R	V	O	I	R	M	J	O	L	P	F	F	N	E	S	N	A	T
Y	S	E	R	T	R	A	D	E	P	I	L	T	A	E	N	I	M	E	Y	A	R
L	E	M	C	O	N	S	E	R	V	A	T	I	O	N	Y	D	O	P	O	R	A
G	O	E	V	I	W	K	S	Y	K	S	I	O	N	A	P	L	S	M	O	G	E
P	I	N	C	I	N	E	R	A	T	O	R	L	I	M	O	B	J	K	T	K	M

Gateway for Geography Name _____

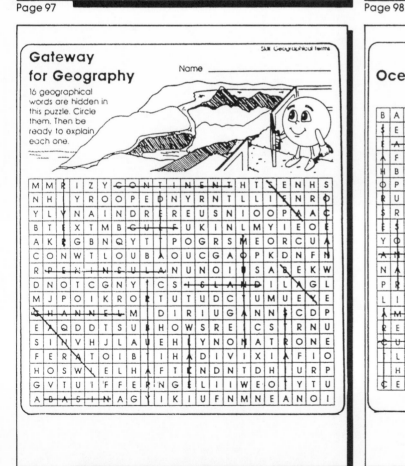

16 geographical words are hidden in this puzzle. Circle them. Then be ready to explain each one.

M	M	R	I	Z	Y	C	O	N	T	I	N	E	N	T	H	T	S	E	N	H	S
N	H		Y	R	O	O	P	E	D	N	Y	R	N	T	L	L	I	F	N	R	O
Y	L	Y	N	A	I	N	D	R	E	R	E	U	S	N	I	O	O	P	A	A	C
B	T	E	X	T	M	B	G	U	L	F	U	K	I	N	L	M	Y	I	E	O	E
A	K	R	G	B	N	Q	Y	T	T	P	O	G	R	S	M	E	O	R	C	U	A
C	O	N	W	T	L	O	U	B	A	O	U	C	G	A	O	P	K	D	N	F	N
R	P	E	N	I	N	S	U	L	A	N	U	N	O	I	U	S	A	B	E	K	W
D	N	O	T	C	G	N	Y	T	C	S	I	S	L	A	N	D	I	L	A	G	L
M	J	P	O	I	K	R	O	R	T	U	T	U	D	C	T	U	M	U	E	Y	E
C	H	A	N	N	E	L	M	I	D	I	R	I	U	G	A	N	N	S	C	D	P
E	A	Q	D	D	T	S	U	B	H	O	W	S	R	E	I	C	S	I	R	N	U
S	I	N	V	H	J	L	A	U	E	H	L	Y	N	O	N	A	T	R	O	N	E
F	E	R	A	T	O	I	B	I	I	H	A	D	I	V	I	X	I	A	F	I	O
H	O	S	W	E	L	H	A	F	T	C	N	D	N	T	D	H	I	U	R	P	
G	V	T	U	I	F	F	E	R	I	N	G	E	L	I	I	W	E	O	T	Y	U
A	B	A	S	I	N	A	G	Y	I	K	I	U	F	N	M	N	E	A	N	O	I

Ocean Motion! Name _____

The ocean is in continuous motion. Dive into the "deep" to find these underwater words.

B	A	C	F	S	E	A	U	R	C	H	I	N	U	M	C
S	E	O	G	E	I	N	A	X	I	N	D	I	A	N	O
E	A	N	T	A	R	C	T	I	C	P	E	O	N	I	R
A	F	T	U	W	L	C	S	R	N	G	C	E	S	A	
H	B	O	E	G	I	A	V	P	M	E	O	T	L		
O	P	N	V	E	A	L	T	W	O	D	E	A	S	A	R
R	U	E	I	D	E	T	L	A	M	A	K	N	I	R	E
S	R	N	D	A	P	L	A	V	E	L	S	O	F	F	E
E	S	T	L	V	I	C	N	O	R	W	D	G	R	I	
Y	O	L	G	O	A	H	T	S	R	A	O	R	M	S	G
A	N	E	M	O	N	E	H	D	Y	I	A	R	B	N	
N	A	M	Y	E	K	B	C	F	L	E	S	P	T	X	E
P	R	I	T	N	T	O	H	P	A	X	Y	H	I	W	L
L	I	S	B	T	O	S	W	A	C	G	F	Y	V	Y	N
A	M	A	R	I	N	E	B	I	O	L	O	G	I	S	T
R	E	K	M	Y	A	R	H	D	K	I	C	J	S	B	O
C	U	R	R	E	N	T	S	W	O	M	T	B	K	W	A
L	U	G	U	L	F	S	T	R	E	A	M	I	A	C	
H	M	D	M	E	L	K	I	P	A	C	I	F	I	C	
C	E	Y	N	S	F	A	T	H	O	M	S	C	E	R	Y

Answer Key

Lost in Space

Name _____

Skill Astronomy Terms

These space words are "out of sight." Can you find them and bring them back? Find out what each one means.

```
C I M Y C I S A N A S T R O N O M Y E D K Y
I M E A D E L I Q R U P E R O K E L S R C T
X E N O L O S I M I I O B A S R G N I O L L
F I E M F E U O D B A A Z I R N B R E L N E
O E L O E S A L U D I N C T I K R A I R S N
T O R S I C F A W X I E Y B G A H V O S I S
E R M P E O S R B E R T G B A B T I B G E J
Y N O W K P R S W E G A T E L L I T E B L U
F L O E F E A Y I T N R E S A R O A I H L F
V E B R I F U S D A S I U L X O B I T E X A
O B S E R V A T O R Y U S E Y A G I R G T O
S W I A V T S E G A V M O L S T E O D A I K
B L F E H O I M J N I Y R I W O L N Y S O U
I A S T R O L O G Y E D O P I X E T A I N P
L E P A O W S K A C N A S T E R O I D N T E
G U N I V E R S E K E E C A H T N A O W N Y
```

Page 101

Time for Measurement

Name _____

Skill Measurement Terms

It's time to learn about measurement. Measure your knowledge by seeing how long it takes you to find 21 measurement terms.

```
H M O I R A U L S E E R U R T C N O M P N O
L S E C O N D S E M A O I T Y A R T F Y P A
A R Y U R N M A B R C S U O D E I O Q U I F
S E R G S C I G Y S T O N E O C A A E T U R
V M I D L G I A S O L B T Y Q U A R T U T E
M I L E E T F I O G A T G R I S L C D M B E
D M O O S I S L S A L A H E L P S Y E M N D
E I M A L A O H Y L Y L I T E R O M R E A G
I E F Y O F A C O L Y E N R S R O I R T D E
C U I B H O U R S O K H C G H U V N F E A P
U H E F E O Y C U N H M H A M G O I A R N O
P D R A T T R U I I W T B I G A E T Y D W U
A T E D R S N T C H U H I T O T W E E K W N
V O C E H W T M O U N C E A U C U A T I N D
G M O N T H O A H U R T W C K I Y S A N N O
E O R A E W H T N T I S S Y A R D W E K A I
```

Page 102